ALL QUIET ON
THE BORDER

The Civil War Era in Greene
County, Pennsylvania

By

D. Kent Fonner

Beach Lake, Pennsylvania

ALL QUIET ON THE BORDER: THE CIVIL WAR
ERA IN GREENE COUNTY, PENNSYLVANIA

ISBN 978-1478290384

Printed in the United States of America

Table of Contents

PREFACE

The history of Greene County during the Civil War era has been an enigma. Tantalizing clues about the region's experience of the war have been published by local historians and genealogists, but no comprehensive synthesis of the records has been attempted since 1865. Samuel Bates, for example, devotes more than a hundred pages to the Civil War; but while he gives a great deal of information about military developments and the names of Greene County men who fought in the conflict, he says little, if anything, about matters on the home front. For Bates, "The war for the suppression of the Rebellion" was "too recent, and the memory of trials endured and hearthstones made desolate is too fresh, to require the telling of how the calls for men were responded to from mansion and cabin in all its [Greene County's] borders."[1] Reverend William Hanna wrote that the Civil War was "the saddest chapter in the history of our beloved country." He believed the episode "so dark that I have seriously thought of passing it over in silence."[2] Andrew Waychoff only provides a few brief glimpses of life in Greene County at that time. Much of what he does say lacks details, such as dates, and reading his material on the subject can be more frustrating than enlightening. L. K. Evans, who served as a Lieutenant in the 1st Pennsylvania Cavalry, and as editor of the county's Republican newspaper had his fingers on the pulse of the community, limits his history to the pioneer period, with a brief chapter on military affairs provided by Major J. B. Morris. More recently, in 1996, Dr. G. Wayne Smith, concentrating his history on the county's development since 1885, devoted a mere three pages to the Civil War.[3] In all fairness to Dr. Smith, however, his research was not intended to be in depth in that era, and anyone interested in reading about the event was expected to consult the earlier historians and records.

The reluctance of the nineteenth-century local historians to tell the whole story, unfortunately, left room over the years for many myths to arise and fill the gap. It was rumored that Greene County was the most supportive area in Pennsylvania for the Southern cause. The Civil War monument in

Waynesburg faced south because that was the direction of the county's sympathies. Scores of Greene County men fled south to enlist in Virginia regiments. Many did, but these were loyal Virginia regiments recruited in the region of the state that became West Virginia in 1863. Instead of supporting these varied myths, recent research supports the thesis that Greene County residents remained strongly loyal to the Union while maintaining their support for the Democratic Party, which often opposed Lincoln and the Republicans on questions relating to how peace with the South could be achieved and the Union restored. It is the intention of the present work to dissipate the myths and provide a more comprehensive narrative about the county's experiences during this turbulent time in our nation's history.

Before relating that story, however, I would like to make a note about the sources. I began collecting material in earnest about Greene County's experience of the Civil War after finding a report in the *Official Records of the War of the Rebellion* of an expedition by United States Provost Marshal troops from Pittsburgh to enforce enrollment for military conscription in Dunkard Township. Much of what I have learned about the county and its people at that time comes from newspaper sources available through the Pennsylvania State University Library. Its collection of Civil War newspapers contains much of interest from newspapers throughout the state, but I especially found a great deal of political news regarding Greene County in newspapers from Pittsburgh, Harrisburg, and Philadelphia. The county remained a Democrat Party stronghold in Pennsylvania throughout the era. State party leaders could always count on a large majority of votes from "Little Greene." More importantly, the collection includes a fairly complete run of *Waynesburg Messenger* newspapers from August 1861 through March 1865. This collection, along with the *Waynesburg Messenger* file on microfilm at the Cornerstone Genealogical Society in Waynesburg and the State Library in Harrisburg, is an invaluable source for Greene County's history in the mid-nineteenth century.

I also owe a large debt to Laurine Williams of Cornerstone for bringing to my attention the "Diary of James Lindsey" and the "Henry Solomon White Diary" in the society's collection. White's diary is quite complete and details his life as a member of Company N, 6th (West) Virginia Infantry. In addition, Cornerstone has available an interesting journal written by Isaac Scherich who served in Company A, 18th Pennsylvania Cavalry.

Along with the Greene County histories that have been published over the past hundred forty years, there have been several studies of Pennsylvania during the Civil War that are especially important in placing Greene County's experiences in context. The most recent of these is Robert M. Sandow, *Deserter Country: Civil War Opposition in the Pennsylvania Appalachians* (Fordham University Press, 2009). Sandow has a great introduction in his book discussing the role of the opposition in the North during the Civil War. His work details events during the war in the Pennsylvania lumbering counties in the north and north-central region of the state. Grace Palladino, *Another Civil War: Labor, Capital, and the State in the Anthracite Regions of Pennsylvania, 1840-1868* (Fordham University Press, 2006), describes Civil War opposition in the coal fields of northeast Pennsylvania. I also found a work by George A. Turner, of Bloomsburg University, titled *Civil War Letters from Soldiers and Citizens of Columbia County, Pennsylvania* (American Heritage Custom Publishing, 1996), quite useful because of some leads he supplied regarding Greene County's position as a region opposing Republican war policies. Finally, Arnold Shankman's book, *The Pennsylvania Antiwar Movement, 1861-1865* (Farleigh Dickinson University Press, 1980), is an important study of Democratic Party opposition to the Republicans from a state-wide perspective.

My investigation into the events described here continues. Along its course I gratefully acknowledge the assistance of many people. Besides Laurine Williams, mentioned above, there are several others at Cornerstone in Waynesburg who have done a great service in preserving the records. These include, among others, Ruth Craft, Malvine Zollars, and Norma T. Bell, all of whom devoted much time to the Cornerstone's research library and its quarterly journal, *Cornerstone Clues*. At the Greene County Historical Society, Brenda Giles, executive director several years ago, gave me invaluable access and guidance to the society library and archives. The Greene County Clerk of Court's Office staff deserve mention for taking time one day to dig out an old criminal case file from the December 1864 term of court. I also wish to acknowledge two of my professors at Waynesburg College, Dr. Thomas Pavick and John Holleran, who taught me much about the historical imagination needed for research in local history. In addition, Candice Buchanan should also be thanked for the fine work she is doing in preserving the county's photographic records at her Greene Connections website, and Jan Slater and Bill Davison should be thanked for their excellent work on the history of slavery and people of color in Greene County. I want to acknowledge my family, including my aunts and uncles who over the years shared many stories about Greene County's past. I want to remember my father and my mother, Henry B. Fonner and Helen Jacobs Fonner, who were always an inspiration to me over the years. I also want to say a word about my daughter, Brittany, now engaged in her own research project in biochemistry at Montana State University, who spent an afternoon with me in Harrisburg, at the Pennsylvania State Library, going through rolls of newspaper microfilm.

Finally, I want to thank my wife, Diane, who has patiently listened to my own stories about Greene County. When I shared with her one day the material I had accumulated on the county's Civil War history, I told her I might put it together into an article or small pamphlet. She looked at the pile of loose leaf notebooks and told me I should write a book. This is what I have done, and for her inspiration, love, and encouragement, I dedicate this work to her.

---

[1] Samuel P. Bates, *History of Greene County, Pennsylvania* (Chicago: Nelson, Rishforth, and Co., 1888), p. 363.

[2] Rev. William Hanna, *History of Greene County, Pa.* (1882), p. 322.

[3] Dr. G. Wayne Smith, *History of Greene County, Pennsylvania* (Morgantown, WV: Cornerstone Genealogical Society of Waynesburg, PA, 1996), pp. 27-29.

Introduction

On the old James Fonner farm, on Fonner Run in Morris Township, during the 1960s, there was a pile of rotten lumber, smothered in brush, in the center of the "Bottom" pasture which was all that remained of what the family called the "old sheep shed." According to family legend, during the Civil War, one of James Fonner's daughters was engaged to a young man who was drafted to serve in the Union army. Fearing for his safety and hoping to keep him from being picked up by the military authorities that were patrolling Morris Township looking for draft dodgers and deserters; she hid him in the sheep shed until the patrols had left the vicinity.

Harboring deserters under the federal draft law passed in 1863 carried a possible penalty of six months to two years imprisonment and a fine not to exceed five hundred dollars,[1] so it would be interesting to know what motivated this young farm girl to risk her freedom and reputation in an act of civil disobedience. One explanation that the family gave was that the Fonners, being Pennsylvania Dutch, were conscientious objectors and opposed to the war on religious grounds. Indeed, on one county enrollment, James Fonner's son, Frederick Fonner, was listed as "exempt" from military service, although no reason was given. There may have been some truth to this explanation, however, since no record of any direct descendant of the James Fonner family serving in the military has been found before the Second World War.

It is just as likely, however, that the Fonners, and their Greene County neighbors, like the residents of many rural counties in Pennsylvania, had mixed emotions about the events of the mid-nineteenth century. The county's position on the Mason-Dixon Line added to those emotions by the fact that many families in the region still had relatives in the South and only a paper border separated the area from potential invasion by hostile secession forces. For the most part, the county reflected the ambivalence of many of the border regions regarding questions of the abolition of slavery and secession. When war started, however, Greene County men generally responded with patriotism and courage. Union rallies were well

1

attended, and in the first year hundreds of Greene County youths volunteered for service in regiments being raised for the Union war effort in Pennsylvania and western Virginia. Women at home formed soldiers' aid societies, and communities raised funds to pay recruits bounties to help support their families while they served. As the war continued, symptoms of war weariness began to grow, and military policies regarding emancipation of slaves in the rebellious parts of the country and military conscription resulted in open resistance to federal authority in some townships.

Like other regions of the North, Greene County became politically divided. There had traditionally been a large majority of the county voters who supported the Democratic Party. In the 1850s, the Whig Party minority was replaced by Republicans after the national Whig Party disintegrated over the slavery issue. By the 1863 and 1864 elections, however, the Democratic Party in the county became divided, with a small minority referring to themselves as "Union" Democrats or War Democrats who supported total war for suppression of the southern rebellion, though they did not necessarily agree with every war measure adopted by the Lincoln administration. These voters eventually formed a coalition with county Republicans to create a Union Party which tended to reduce the Democrat Party election majorities in Greene County. The remainder of the Democratic Party, and the majority, became known as Peace Democrats who openly opposed many of Lincoln's war measures, including the Emancipation Proclamation, ratification of the Thirteenth Amendment to abolish slavery, and the national military conscription law. These Democrats stood firmly for "the Constitution as it is" and "the Union as it was." Until almost the very end of the war, Greene County Peace Democrats, like Peace Democrats throughout the North, called for a negotiated settlement with the South.

Political divisiveness, reflected in county newspapers, led to increasing assaults and violence between extreme factions of all parties. Military draft resistance brought federal troops into the county to enforce enrollment under the conscription law. Rumors of potential violence and operations by Knights of the Golden Circle brought federal troops into the county on other occasions to investigate, arrest draft evaders and deserters, and stand guard over election polls. Tensions over military conscription reached a point where one Perry Township resident, evading the government agents, shot and killed his neighbor.

In the meantime, as many Greene County men served in the armies fighting in the South, the region experienced life on the home front. Waynesburg residents began thinking about municipal parks and fire-fighting equipment. Oil was discovered on Dunkard Creek. Agriculture continued as the major economic activity in the county. Stock raising had always been important to Greene County farmers. During the Civil War era, sheep and wool production took on even more importance. Transportation remained a difficulty yet to be resolved; but by the end of the war, dreams of imminent railroads fueled the imaginations of county merchants and lawyers. Before the end of the war, a new county map was published showing a complete picture of the roads, communities, property owners, and businesses of the region. As the war came to a close, Greene County residents looked to the future with hope. In a few short years after the war, the county witnessed an oil and gas boom, the construction of the Waynesburg and Washington Railroad, and the expansion of Waynesburg Borough and Waynesburg College. At the turn of the twentieth century, a coal land boom rocked the foundations of the region's economic growth. As the county's history was being written in the midst of these developments in the last quarter of the nineteenth century, it is little wonder that minimal attention was paid to the domestic troubles of the recent past.

The present study originally began as an investigation of antiwar sentiment in Greene County during the Civil War, but continued research has led to the conclusion that such an approach bought into earlier myths about Greene County's "southern" sympathies. The evidence indicates that the county was not so much divided over support for the Union but more importantly on how that support should be expressed. There are records to indicate that an infinitesimal segment of the population, probably in the southern most townships, had sympathy for the southern cause. The vast majority of Greene County residents, however, were loyal Unionists. Nevertheless,

3

the various factions each had formed a different definition of "loyalty." For county Republicans, loyalty to the Union required unquestioning support for Abraham Lincoln and the Republicans in Congress. They demanded that opponents accept all the war policies of the Lincoln administration or be branded as traitors. To win elections, they were willing to turn down their rhetoric and cooperate with War Democrats through the Union Leagues and the Union Party. The War Democrats, in turn, although not necessarily agreeing with all Lincoln's policies, were willing to concede the necessity of some policies, such as abolition of slavery, as a war measure to strike at the root of rebellion. Republicans denounced Peace Democrats as disloyal "copperheads." The Peace Democrats, probably about two thirds of the county, were Unionist in sentiment, but they opposed much of Lincoln's policy, especially abolition, military conscription, suspension of *habeas corpus,* and martial law. They sought an end to the conflict and restoration of the Union based on some compromise, such as that proposed by Kentucky Senator John J. Crittenden in December 1860. For them, Republicans were abolitionists and traitors. Supporters of many Lincoln policies were viewed as enemies of the Constitution. Greene County in the Civil War era, therefore, presented "a house divided." The county, consequently, could not remain a quiet spot on the border, despite the idyllic face that has shown to us across the steep hollow of time.

---

[1] *Waynesburg Messenger,* 29 July 1863, p. 3.

Chapter I: To "Halt Between Two Opinions"

Located on the southwest corner of the state, Greene County, Pennsylvania, was once described as "a monotonously hilly region lying a little aside from any of the great natural transcontinental routes of travel and the transportation facilities are limited."[1] Certainly, transportation, or, more likely, the difficulty thereof, "has ever been a significant factor in the county's history."[2] By 1860, the region had been bypassed by two major nineteenth-century transportation systems. The National Road skirted Greene County in the north, passing from Uniontown, Fayette County, through Brownsville on the Monongahela River, through Washington, Pennsylvania, to Wheeling, Virginia, on the Ohio River. Below the Mason-Dixon Line, which forms the area's southern border, the B&O Railroad ran across western Virginia to Parkersburg, Virginia, on the Ohio River, with a branch proceeding through the panhandle of western Virginia to Wheeling.

The Monongahela River forms the county's eastern border; and this river was Greene County's easiest access to the outside world. Since the early days of settlement, there developed three main forms of river transportation—the flatboat, which could only navigate downstream with the current, the keelboat, powered by boatmen pushing long poles against the river bottom, allowing slow movement upstream as well as down, and, by 1850, the steam-powered, paddle-wheeled, riverboat. A series of locks and dams built under the charter of the Monongahela Navigation Company, including one at Rices Landing, by 1856, made "slack water" navigation possible from Pittsburgh to that point and Greensboro in Monongahela Township. In 1859, three steamboats making regular runs on the Monongahela River between Pittsburgh and Greensboro were the *Telegraph,* captained by J. C. Woodward, the *Jefferson,* commanded by Captain George Clark, and Captain H. Bennett's boat, the *Luzerne.* At that time, passengers from Pittsburgh to Uniontown paid a fare of two dollars, including meals and a state room on a boat. Stops were made at various landings along the river, including McKeesport, Elizabethtown, Monongahela City, Cookstown, Millsborough, Rice's Landing, Greensboro, and Geneva.[3] By the spring of 1864, the steamboat, *Telegraph,* was popular with travelers between New Geneva and Brownsville. Her captain, Doyle Bugher, was "one of the oldest and most trustworthy Pilots on the River." Other officers included Robert McIntire as First Mate, Second Mate Isaiah Walters, Isaac Cooper as First Engineer, and N. Carpenter as Second Engineer. The office staff was Jeremiah H. Carmack, assisted by Robert Lynch, "accomplished and efficient Clerks," who were "courteous, obliging, prompt, and accurate."[4]

During the war, travel by riverboat to recruit camps near Pittsburgh became a novelty for hundreds of Greene County men. D. S. Hopkins remembered that the trip down the Monongahela River was "our first boat ride." He wrote that "the day was rather pleasant and the senary[sic] was grand and all things considered the trip was pleasant and we enjoyed it very much."[5] When Captain William Lindsey's recruits for Company A, Eighteenth Pennsylvania Cavalry, made the trip from Rice's Landing, one recruit, Isaac Scherich, related that all of the men, except three, became drunk on whiskey provided by a local distillery owner, Bill Sedgewick. Scherich noted:

> They sure had a hot time going down the river that night. The water in the river was very low and the boat ran aground several times. What those drunken men did not do was not much. Many of them left all the good dinner that the people of Jefferson had given them on the deck of the boat or threw it overboard to feed the fishes.
>
> Billy Martin and I, to get away from the jambouree[sic], crawled out onto a raft of logs, which the boat had in tow, and went to sleep, when we awoke we were very cold, from the effects of which, we each suffered for several days from a severe cold in the head. It took more than twenty hours to go about sixty miles downstream.

The boat landed at Port Perry, about twelve miles from Pittsburgh, and Scherich and his companions continued their journey by rail.[6] The riverboat, *Elector,* transporting the "Greene County Rifles" to Pittsburgh ran aground on sandbars more than once. At one point, the men had to wade ashore and walk for several miles until the worst of the sandbars had been passed.[7]

A hack, carrying mail and passengers, owned by Timothy Dougher, ran regularly between the county seat at Waynesburg and Rice's Landing on the river.[8] Travelers could daily leave the Hamilton House in Waynesburg at seven thirty in the morning and Rice's Landing at one o'clock in the afternoon. Dougher was known as a "good-natured . . . enterprising and accommodating coachman."[9] When river transportation was closed due to ice in the winter, Dougher ran daily sleighs to Brownsville, where passengers could then connect with coaches to Uniontown. This was noted as "the cheapest and most expeditious route to Pittsburgh during suspension of navigation."[10] As the war progressed, in 1864, Dougher expanded his business to three coaches and ten to twelve horses. The coaches were said to have been "snugly refitted, new harness bought, and no effort spared to make the trip to the Landing and back a downright comfort in any sort of endurable weather."[11] During the war, Dougher's Waynesburg and Rice's Landing Stage Company provided transportation to the Quartermaster General's Office in Washington, D.C., for "Recruits, Deserters, etc." From November 1864 to June 1865, Dougher claimed $180.75 in payment for his services to the army.[12] Another stage coach line connected Greensboro and Morgantown.[13]

The river being the surest transportation route for business and commercial travel, many residents of Greene County, who did not live close to the Monongahela, remained on isolated farms and villages, seldom traveling more than a few miles from home, with an occasional trip to Waynesburg, the county seat, Washington, Pennsylvania, or nearby towns like Cameron in western Virginia. By the 1860s, Greene County's road system, as demonstrated on J. L. McConnell's map published in 1865, was well established. The conditions of these roads, however, were often deplorable. One Lancaster

County writer noted that the Greene County papers reported that "the road between Waynesburg and Rice's Landing is worse than it was ever known before." He added, "It must be bad."[14] When advertising for bids for conveying the mail, in 1864, the Post Office Department calculated five hours for a contractor to make the twelve-mile trip from Waynesburg to Rice's Landing.[15] In the summer of 1858, Dr. David W. Gray of Richhill Township was seriously injured when the horse pulling the sulky he was riding bolted and "ran for some distance over the rough and stony road" from Jacktown to Ryerson's Station, "and striking a stump upset the sulky."[16] By the spring of 1862, it was reported that Greene County's "country roads are in a shocking condition." The road between Waynesburg and Rice's Landing was "almost impassable." The *Messenger* blamed the condition of the roads on the failure of the township supervisors to make necessary repairs in the summer months. "Neglect of this kind is utterly inexcusable," wrote the editors, "and supervisors who fail in their duty are a positive nuisance."[17] The Waynesburg Turnpike Road Company was chartered by the state in March 1859. The road ran from the mouth of Bates Fork in Franklin Township through Waynesburg east to Morrisville and then to Rices Landing. L. K. Evans, however, dismissed the project as "an ungraded mud pike, almost impassible half the year."[18] In 1865, an investor in the Greene County Amber Oil Company observed that roads to farms purchased as oil properties "were impassable six months in a year, and break-neck concerns at the best of times." In describing one property known as the "Clark Farm," the investor stated that there was "some bottom land," but that residents in the area told him no one would "give $5,000 for any farm in the country around" since "no one can raise crops there, for they are all washed down the hills by the rains."[19]

This isolation and disappointment over the failure of the county to find the same commercial advantages as their neighbors in southwestern Pennsylvania led eventually to a growing resentment for, and suspicion of, strangers. Since the days of the Whiskey Rebellion, in 1794, the residents of Greene County were especially wary of the Federal government. Being bounded by Virginia on the west and the south, and at one time claimed as a part of Virginia until the final establishment of the

Mason-Dixon Line, it is not surprising that Greene County seemed more closely tied to western Virginia than Pennsylvania. Many of the oldest families in the area had migrated from Virginia and Maryland, with a seasoning of Pennsylvania Dutch from eastern Pennsylvania, who crossed the mountains over the Forbes Road. The nineteenth-century local historian, Reverend William Hanna, states that citizens of Greene County "were ever on the alert watching for an action of the general government that had the appearance of *sectionalism*."[20] Many thought they saw, in the winter of 1860-61, "an effort to coerce the southern states, and interfere with their domestic institution."[21] As a result, the majority of political leaders and residents of the county in early 1861 hesitated in deciding their loyalties.

Although at least two routes for the Underground Railroad have been identified in Greene County,[22] the people were ambivalent about the slavery issue. As one historian noted, "Down until the close of the ante-bellum period this region illustrated well the independence or division of opinion of the whole border territory on the issue of slavery."[23] Greene County residents had never owned many slaves. Census records indicate twenty-two slaves in 1800; ten slaves in 1810; and seven slaves in 1820. In 1820, two hundred fifty-four free Blacks lived in the county.[24] In 1860, the free Black population had increased slightly to three hundred fifteen. The census also listed two hundred eleven mulattoes for a total "free colored" population of five hundred twenty-six. Of this number, forty-seven resided in Franklin Township and fifty in Marion Township, which included the limits of Waynesburg.[25] A meeting of Washington Township Democrats, in 1863, voiced the views of many county residents. In one resolution, they condemned with "our utter abhorrence" both the "'impartial freedom' for negroes as taught by the abolitionists of the North, and 'Secession' as taught by the fire-eaters of the South."[26]

A portion of the residents of Waynesburg and the nearby village of Dodysburg, east of town, became quite vocal in their opinions about their Black neighbors in the summer of 1859. That summer had started badly for the county when it was found on the morning of June 5, 1859, that a late heavy frost had blighted the growing wheat crop throughout the region.

According to Reverend Hanna, the loss of the wheat crop that summer was accompanied by "dark, gloomy and awful . . . forebodings of many with reference to the question, 'What shall we eat?'"[27] The remaining flour in the county was soon subject to market speculation as some bought up enough of a supply at exuberant prices to last a year and others sought to profit from the misfortune of their neighbors by pricing their remaining stock of flour at double its pre-frost cost. More than a few refused to sell at any price. A Gettysburg newspaper reported, "The late frost produced all the more consternation in Western Pennsylvania, from the general scarcity of grain, and speculators anticipated immense profits."[28] Calls were made for grain distilleries in the region to stop operation, and many voluntarily ceased work as soon as the day of the frost. More than that, several operators began selling their remaining stock of grain in small quantities to their destitute neighbors at cost. In Greene County, William Gray, owner of a distillery in Monongahela Township, was selling corn at ninety cents a bushel while some farmers in the area were asking $1.25.[29] The cashier of the Farmers and Drovers Bank in Waynesburg, Jesse Lazear, sought to relieve fears of famine by obtaining buckwheat seed for a later planting. He then sold the seed to the community's farmers in amounts limited to one bushel per family. Anyone not able to pay for the seed was given seed on credit.[30]

A Greene County speculator, John Patterson, purchased a quantity of wheat and had on hand at Rush's Mill, in the edge of Washington County, about eighty barrels of flour. After the frost hit, Patterson was asking fifteen dollars per barrel for his flour. About two weeks later, in open daylight on a Friday, about fifty men and twenty teams of horses drove in procession to the mill, hauled away Patterson's flour, and left payment for it at the rate of eight dollars a barrel. The Greene County men then divided the flour and distributed it to those in the vicinity who were considered the neediest. It seems that the mob included some of the most respected citizens of that part of the county. Public sentiment justified the action as necessary to prevent famine, especially since it had been reported that Patterson was seeking to sell the flour in Wheeling. The crowd also seized a stock of wheat owned by Patterson, stored at another place, and disposed of it in a similar way.[31]

By August, tensions in Dodysburg, near Waynesburg, ran high as some of the White residents of the area, apparently, began to share the belief that "the presence of the negroes in the neighborhood tended to lower the price of labor." A gang of Dodysburg men decided that the village should be rid of its Black population, and they warned their neighbors to leave. One of the Dodysburg toughs, Allen Herrington, told patrons in Huffman's blacksmith shop in Dodysburg that "the colored people were here, working for little or nothing, and he intended to run them all out." Andrew Lantz, a White resident of Dodysburg, was told by Job Morris, Allen Herrington, and George Wisecarver that "they were determined to run all the darkies out of the land." They also told him "to move Seaton," his Black employee. Lantz added, "They told me there should never be another colored man work on my place." According to Lantz, "they ran Seaton out; they said they would beat them all till they left."

The Blacks refused to vacate their homes, procured arms, and made preparations for their own defense. Daniel Ditcher, a Black resident who operated a barber shop in Waynesburg, told one patron that if the Dodysburg men were not "careful they would have bleeding Kansas here." On the evening of August 25, 1859, a mob of these White residents of the village were in Waynesburg. One of them, a man named William Seeley Zimmerman, argued with Ditcher on the steps of the Hamilton House, where Ditcher's barber shop was located. Zimmerman offered to bet Ditcher five or ten dollars that "him or no other black son-of-a-bitch could go through Dotysburg[sic] the next day." Ditcher replied that if he had business in Dodysburg, he would go and defend himself if anyone tried to "molest him." One man present warned Zimmerman "that the Negroes were armed to the teeth." Zimmerman insisted that he was not afraid and that he "intended to make a clear sweep of all he seen on the street that night." John Hoge remembered that Zimmerman later came by the well where he was working and told Thomas J. Kent that he and his boys "were going to drive all the d---d niggers out of town or kill them." "We have drove them all off from our place," he said, "and we intended to from Waynesburg." At the

11

bar at the Green House, run by Shadrach Sellers, Zimmerman "swore they intended to kill from a half dozen to a dozen niggers that night." As Zimmerman and his gang made their way uptown, a witness heard one of the crowd say, "Let's go into the Barber shop and if there are any niggers there we will hoist them." Another witness heard Zimmerman say that "he would either kill a nigger that night or be killed himself." Another member of the crowd, named McVey, "said he intended to have a nigger's scalp that night." During the course of their rampage in town, Zimmerman knocked down a Black man named Monroe in the street, while members of his gang "were rather abusive in their remarks about the colored people of the place."

They returned to Dodysburg about ten o'clock that night, Zimmerman expressing a desire to give "old Alf [Alfred Wells, a free Black resident of the village] a round." As Zimmerman's toughs crossed an area known as "Hook's Field," they were suddenly attacked by a band of fifteen or twenty Blacks. Twelve or fourteen shots were fired. As the Whites fled in the darkness, one man, Allen Herrington, was wounded in the arm. Zimmerman was killed, and the Blacks, "satisfied with the results of the conflict, returned to their homes." The next day, eight Black residents of Dodysburg were arrested for the murder of Zimmerman. When trial was held in the Greene County court, two of the men, Alfred Wells and Henry Suttles, were acquitted and six--Daniel Ditcher, William Workman, Daniel Clifford, Robert Suttles, George Seaton, and James Workman--were found guilty of manslaughter. Each of the convicted men was sentenced to five years and nine months in the Western Penitentiary in Allegheny County.[32] After the verdict, "there was considerable dissatisfaction exhibited upon the street by noisy demonstrations, with drum and fife and transparency stigmatizing the jury—and concluding by burning them in effigy." The *Waynesburg Messenger*, acknowledging the difference in opinions about the verdict, reminded the citizens of their duty to obey the law.[33] On February 6, 1860, Dr. David W. Gray, from Richhill Township, Greene County's representative in the Pennsylvania House, introduced a petition "for a law to prevent the immigration of free blacks into this state."[34]

Reverend Hanna summed up the view of most Greene County citizens as war approached between North and South in 1861:

> They said if we were sure that the intention is to maintain the integrity of the Union," we would accept the situation and assist in crushing out the rebellion;" but if the intention is to wage a war against slaveholders for the purpose of liberating the colored race who (in their opinion) did not desire freedom, "Then we are not ready to assist." This uncertainty with reference to the intentions of the leaders [of the Union], caused many to "halt between two opinions."[35]

[1] Ralph W. Stone and Frederick G. Clapp, *Oil and Gas Fields of Greene County, Pa.* (Washington, D.C.: Government Printing Office, 1907), p. 8.

[2] *Inventory of the County Archives of Pennsylvania: Greene County*, #30, Prepared by the Pennsylvania Historical Records Survey Division of Professional and Service Projects, Works Projects Administration (Waynesburg, PA: Board of County Commissioners, 1940), p. 15.

[3] *Pittsburgh Daily Gazette and Advertiser*, 29 January 1859, p. 3.

[4] *Waynesburg Messenger* (Waynesburg, PA), 4 May 1864, p. 3.

[5] D. S. Hopkins, "Reminiscence of My Service in the U. S. Army from 26th Day of February 1864 to 11th Day of July 1865," handwritten manuscript, PA Historical & Museum Commission, Division of Archives and Manuscripts, MG-6-Diaries and Journals-Box #1, p. 1.

[6] "The 18th Pennsylvania Rides Again!!," a transcription of the memoirs/journal of Private Isaac Scherich, Company A, 18th Pennsylvania Cavalry (available at the Cornerstone Genealogical Society, Waynesburg, Pa.), pp. 2-3. The original of Isaac Scherich's journal is in the Trans-Appalachian Room of the Waynesburg University Library, Waynesburg, PA.

[7] Professor Robert Laird Stewart, D.D., *History of the One Hundred and Fortieth Regiment Pennsylvania Volunteers* (published by authority of the regimental association, 1912), p. 291.

[8] *Waynesburg Messenger*, 6 February 1861, p. 3.

[9] *Waynesburg Messenger*, 23 October 1861, p. 3.

[10] *Ibid*, 13 January 1864, p. 3.

[11] *Ibid*, 2 March 1864, p. 3.

[12] Photocopy of Letter from Col. Alexander Rush, in charge of 4th Division, Quartermaster Department, to Honorable G. V. Lawrence, House of Representatives, Washington, D.C., dated 14 December 1866 (private collection of D. Kent Fonner, Beach Lake, PA; original in the archive collection of the Greene County Historical Society, Waynesburg, PA).

[13] *Pittsburgh Daily Gazette and Advertiser*, 29 January 1859, p. 3.

[14] *Lancaster Intelligencer*, 18 May 1870, p. 2.

[15] *The Franklin Repository* (Chambersburg, PA), 17 February 1864, p. 9.

[16] *Daily Morning Post*, 20 August 1858, p. 3.

[17] *Waynesburg Messenger*, 5 March 1862, p. 3.

[18] L. K. Evans, *Pioneer History of Greene County*, p. 132.

[19] *The Press* (Philadelphia), 28 August 1865, p. 4.

[20] Rev. William Hanna, *History of Greene County* (1882), p. 323.

[21] *Ibid.*

[22] Andrew J. Waychoff, *Local History of Greene County and Southwestern Pennsylvania* (1994 reprint by Cornerstone Genealogical Society, Waynesburg, PA), pp. 28, 50.

[23] Alfred P. James, "The Significance of Western Pennsylvania in American History," *Western Pennsylvania Historical Magazine*, Vol. 16, No. 4 (November 1933), p. 276.

[24] Marie Elaine Powell, "All These Munificent Gifts . . . the Social and Economic Development of Greene County, Pennsylvania 1760-1976" (unpublished manuscript of Honors Project submitted to Denison University, 5 May 1976), (Waynesburg, PA: Greene County Historical Society Collection), pp. 76, 100.

[25] Joseph C. G. Kennedy, Superintendent of Census, *Population of the United States in 1860; Compiled from the Original Returns of the Eighth Census under Direction of the Secretary of the Interior* (Washington: Government Printing Office, 1864), pp. 412, 424.

[26] *The Waynesburg Messenger*, 6 May 1863, p. 1.

[27] Hanna, p. 105.

[28] *Republican Compiler* (Gettysburg, PA), 27 June 1859, p. 3.

[29] *Pittsburgh Daily Gazette and Advertiser*, 25 June 1859, p. 2.

[30] Powell, p. 72.

[31] *Republican Compiler* (Gettysburg), 27 June 1859, p. 3.

[32] *The Press* (Philadelphia), 11 January 1860, p.2. Also see *The Waynesburg Messenger,* 29 December 1859 (transcribed by Bill A. Davison, http://home.comcast.net/~janslater/Waynesburg_Messenger_Trial_Coverage .htm, retrieved 8/21/2011).

[33] *The Waynesburg Messenger*, 29 December 1859 (transcribed by Bill A. Davison, ibid).

[34] *Philadelphia Press*, 7 February 1860, p. 2.

[35] Hanna, P. 323.

Home Front Vignette: "Map of Greene County"

[The J. L. McConnell Map of Greene County published in 1865 was probably one of the most accurate and detailed maps published of the county made available to the general public until the appearance of the Caldwell Atlas of Greene County in 1876. The McConnell Map provided a great deal of information about the residents and businesses of Greene County in the 1860s, as well as the geographical and political boundaries of the county's communities. On February 1, 1865, the Waynesburg Messenger published an item describing the origins and upcoming availability of this map to its readers.]

"Our readers will remember that some four or five years since, our county was very accurately surveyed, with a view to publishing a county map. The war breaking out shortly after, the gentlemen who had undertaken the enterprise, gave it up, very much to the regret of many of our people. We are much pleased, therefore, to learn that the project is now renewed under the auspices of Joseph L. McConnell, Esq., of this county. A friend now in Philadelphia, in speaking of this matter says: –

'Your people or many of them, at least, will be rejoiced to learn that, after long waiting, we are certainly to have a large, accurate and beautiful map of Greene Co. This is no longer a matter of doubt. It has become one of the 'fixed facts' of the day. I have had the pleasure of examining the skeleton of this map, before it was put into the hands of the engravers, and, so far as I am capable of judging, I believe it to be very perfect, – showing all the streams, woods, Township lines, and in fact the residences of all the land-owners in the County. Our people will be indebted to Joseph L. McConnell, Esq., for this valuable work. He has recently purchased the surveys made by Simon J. Martinets, Esq., of Baltimore, in the year 1859, and after making all necessary corrections, has now the work in the hands of the engravers; and by next March court, it is expected to have this important work ready for sale. Mr. McConnell has been spending the last two or three weeks in the city superintending this map at private expense, and I sincerely hope his enterprise and energy may meet with the reward he merits.

He learned – I don't now remember where – that there is another party – I don't know who – endeavoring to get up a Map of Greene County. The public will do well, however, to wait for the map by Mr. McConnell, – for there isn't a man in the state better calculated than he to make a true and accurate map of the County.'

Very respectfully, etc., P."

Chapter II: "A Speck of War in Greene County"

Dr. G. Wayne Smith, in his *History of Greene County*, states unequivocally that "Greene County strongly supported the Union during the Civil War."[1] In his "Centennial Address" on "Greene County's Military Record," delivered in 1896, Major J. B. Morris observed:

> The patriotism of the inhabitants of Greene County has never been questioned. Every man and woman felt proud of our growing republic and when news came that the flag of the country had been fired on at Fort Sumter, a universal feeling of indignation was publicly expressed. Men forgot their political opinions, and when the call for men and means came, Greene County was prompt to respond.[2]

After the Battle of Shiloh, Major General Don Carlos Buell, commander of the Army of the Ohio, had a member of his staff call attention to the good conduct of four men from the Anderson Troop, a Pennsylvania cavalry battalion present as headquarters' guards. One of these, Private J. Randolph Hewitt, was from Carmichaels, Greene County. In a letter to Hewitt's captain, William J. Palmer, Buell's assistant adjutant general, J. M. Wright, described "the gallant manner in which during the hottest of the fight," Hewitt and his companion, Private Smith from Philadelphia, "rallied scattered parties of men and led them back to their regiments" making both of them "deserving of the highest commendations."[3] Dr. Smith cites two Greene Countians, James Jackson Purman and James M. Pipes, who received the Congressional Medal of Honor. More recent research has identified four additional men from Greene County awarded the Medal of Honor, including William E. Leonard, from Jacksonville (now Wind Ridge) in Richhill Township, John Shanes from Brave, Charles A. Swan, while serving in Company K, Fourth Iowa Cavalry, and Andrew J. Young from

Carmichaels.[4] . No record has been found of any person from Greene County who served in a military unit of the Confederate States.[5]

To the contrary, after Virginia passed its secession resolution and word was received that secessionist Virginia forces were occupying Clarksburg, in western Virginia, a Greene County correspondent to the *Pennsylvania Daily Telegraph* in Harrisburg, identified as "Sentinal," commented on "the consternation which prevailed everywhere throughout the county, simply because we have no means of defence [sic] should the enemy attack." Referring to the Virginia secessionist forces as "hordes of mercenaries and savages," he condemned the governor of Pennsylvania for failing to take proper measures to protect Greene County's "towns and villages almost within sight of the Virginia line." "All that we ask," he wrote, "are the arms and ammunition. We have the hands and shoulders here to bear them, as well as the courage and ability to defend our wives and children and homes from the assault of our foes."[6]

When Grafton, on the B&O Railroad, was occupied by rebel forces, the citizens of Morgantown feared an attack on the night of May 27, 1861. The authorities promptly sent messages to Greene County, Fayette County, and Pittsburgh, in Pennsylvania, asking for assistance. The response from Fayette and Greene counties was overwhelming. *The Genius of Liberty* noted that the news caused "the greatest excitement, enthusiasm and alarm . . . to take hold of our citizens." Local government officials held meetings with residents and militia units while arms were secured for defense of the border.[7] One Fayette County farmer noted that the alarm spread through Fayette and Greene "like lightning." By the morning, "a multitude was in march for Morgantown." "All the next day," he wrote to *The Press* in Philadelphia, "companies were forming and commencing their march in the direction of that place."[8] Excitement rose, and "men of all ages abandoned their usual pursuits, and in a few minutes were on their way to some appointed place of rendezvous."[9] As numerous Pennsylvania men arrived in Morgantown, and with hundreds more on the roads from Waynesburg and Uniontown, the alarm was allayed with word that the rebels had retreated from Grafton following the approach of Federal forces from Wheeling and the Ohio

River under command of General George McClellan. As the *Genius of Liberty* reported:

> Although these demonstrations in one sense, may seem to have been unnecessary, yet they have been highly important in showing the loyalty and patriotism of our citizen soldiery, and the promptness with which they responded to the call of duty, and also in more closely cementing the bonds of union and fraternal feeling among our citizens of Pennsylvania and Western Virginia.[10]

When Washington County's Ringgold Cavalry was called into active service and directed to report to Grafton in western Virginia on the B&O Railroad, the militiamen assembled at Beallsville and rode toward the south on June 22, 1861. They spent their first night on the march at Carmichaels, where it was noted by the regimental historian that "the men were hospitably entertained in the homes of the citizens." The next day, the company of seventy men proceeded toward Morgantown. When the men reached the point where the road between Carmichaels and Morgantown crossed the border into western Virginia, they found a large United States flag suspended across the state line. Captain Keyes brought the unit to a halt, and the men gave three loud cheers for the Union before leaving Greene County and riding on.[11]

During the course of the war, as Reverend Hanna explained, "Many of the sons and brothers of Greene County offered themselves as willing sacrifices for their country's good."[12] Motivated by a number of circumstances and emotions, "multitudes from this county pressed forward to fill up the ranks of the Union army."[13] The express sentiment of General Francis A. Walker, the nineteenth-century historian of the Second Corps of the Army of the Potomac, is as true in this century as it was in his. From the perspective of the post-war years, General Walker stated:

> It is difficult at this time, it was difficult even in 1865, to go back to the sentiments and feelings which moved the citizen soldiery of 1861-1862, before custom

had staled the ideas of patriotic sacrifice and martial glory; before long delays and frequent disappointments had robbed war of its romance; before the curse of conscription had come, to make the uniform a thing of doubtful honor, and to substitute the "bounty jumper" for the generous volunteer; while yet all the soldiers in the field were those who sprang to arms in that great uprising of a free people.[14]

William Silveus enlisted in Company I, 8th Pennsylvania Reserve Infantry, on August 25, 1862. His motive for enlisting remains a puzzle. Governor Curtin of Pennsylvania had called for a military draft of eligible men in the state in the late summer of 1862, so it is possible that Silveus enlisted to avoid the stigma of being a conscript or because of a sense of duty to voluntarily do his part to serve the community. Silveus was nearly twenty-eight years old at the time, married, with two very young daughters. Not long after being mustered into the service at Harrisburg, he wrote a letter home telling his wife, Mary Silveus, and his brother, Joe Silveus, that he had "25 dollars that I want to send home as soon as I can." In addition, he reminded them both that they could draw his "County bounty" from the Treasurer as soon as he got an order from the Captain.[15] After the initial rush of volunteers in the summer and fall of 1861, many communities began experiencing difficulty meeting enlistment quotas set by the state government to fill requests by the War Department. The bounty system, initially established as an expression of citizens' gratitude to soldiers for their service, quickly became a perceived solution to the problem by offering a financial incentive for recruits. The amounts varied in different communities, but generally they were high enough to be tempting to a private soldier earning eleven to sixteen dollars per month. Pennsylvania's decision to use a military draft as a means of meeting the nation's need for further troops stimulated recruiting in Greene County. On July 30, 1862, the *Waynesburg Messenger* called for a volunteer company to "be organized promptly, and composed of the best material in the county—brave, stalwart lads, who will give a good account of themselves before the enemy." The newspaper also urged any who were unable to enlist themselves to "give liberally of their means to support" the wives, children, and parents of the new recruits.[16]

R. L. McConnell, A. A. Purman, and J. A. J. Buchanan all spoke at a war meeting held at Gray's Old Stand in Richhill Township. The speakers called for immediate action by enlisting volunteers and providing money "to assist in inducing men to enlist" and to "provide for their families." Among the various activities and speeches at the meeting, including entertainment by the Waynesburg Band led by the Recorder of Deeds, Justus F. Temple, a resolution was passed calling for the County Commissioners to pay Fifty Dollars from the county funds as a bounty to each new recruit. In the event that the Commissioners refused the request, "a subscription" was "started to raise" private donations for "a liberal Bounty for each Volunteer from the county under the late call."[17] One correspondent to the *Messenger,* identified as "Jackson," urged young men of the county to "do voluntarily what otherwise you may be compelled to do!"[18] War meetings at Rogersville and Nineveh in August also recommended the appropriation of county funds for payment of a bounty to each new volunteer. Reviewing recent recruiting activities in Greene County, the *Messenger,* on August 20, 1862, reported that if "the means are raised by subscription or are appropriated by the Commissioners to bounty the volunteers, there will be no trouble, we apprehend, in raising the quota of troops from Greene County without drafting."[19]

The Greene County Commissioners decided to pay a bounty of Fifty Dollars to each new recruit who enlisted prior to September 1, 1862, when the state military draft was scheduled to begin. The decision was endorsed by a county war meeting held at Waynesburg on August 23, 1862.[20] Accordingly, the Treasurer paid out $26,665.00 as bounties to soldiers recruited from Greene County in 1862.[21] It was noted that private individuals in Jefferson Township had subscribed $860.00 for bounties to volunteers and that $900.00 was paid to eighteen men who volunteered in Jefferson in September 1862.[22] In early 1863, Pennsylvania state senator, Amos R. Boughter, Republican from the Fifteenth District (Dauphin and Lebanon Counties), introduced a bill to allow Greene County commissioners to levy a special tax to pay bounties to volunteers. The bill was eventually referred to the state senate Judiciary Committee with instructions to report a general tax bill that could be applied to all Pennsylvania counties.[23] The next year, the Pennsylvania state senate debated legislation regarding payment of bounties for recruits in Morgan Township, Greene County.[24]

Indeed, as the war continued and volunteering began to waiver, many communities raised the amount of these bounties as a means of encouraging recruitment and lowering military conscription quotas. When the federal draft was started in 1863, the national government authorized a bounty of $302 for each new recruit and $402 for each veteran who reenlisted. On November 28, 1863, a community meeting was held in the Greene County Courthouse to discuss ways and means of stimulating volunteering to avoid a second federal draft in the county. The meeting recommended that the county authorize a bounty of $200 to be paid from county funds. It was also noted that the County Relief Board should "make ample provision for the destitute families of soldiers."[25] The citizens of Centre Township offered a private bounty of $100 for recruits and advertised that application could be made with the treasurer, John Kent, in Rogersville, or with the county recruiting agent, T. H. Meighen, at the Hamilton House in Waynesburg. In addition to Centre Township, Jackson, Washington, and Richhill Townships also decided to offer private bounties for recruits.[26] By March of 1864, T. H. Meighen advertised that he could pay $250 in local bounties for new recruits in addition to the federal bounty of $302, making a total of $552 in bounties for each new recruit. "This is certainly a great inducement to patriotic young men to go, and help our brothers in the field," noted Meighen, "and I hope they will respond, and save those of the draft, who have made such liberal contributions."[27] In addition to bounties, the U. S. district provost marshal in 1864 was offering to pay to any non-commissioned officer, private, or citizen who procured an acceptable recruit   enlistment fees of fifteen dollars for each new recruit and twenty-five dollars for veterans.[28]

William Silveus reached the 8th Pennsylvania Reserves while the regiment was still camped on the battlefield at

Antietam. On September 20, 1862, he wrote to his wife that when he reached the regiment, he was greeted by her brother, Albert Mildred. He described how he went over the battlefield that morning, and "O what a sight it was." He counted "as high as thirteen rebels all in one pile," with the dead "scattered for two or three miles." He added, "I never want to witness another such a sight." He seemed to gain some measure of comfort "setting by the side of Albert a writing this letter to you, while he is writing to Mother." To his brother Joe, he described the battlefield as "the awfullest sight that I ever saw and God forbid that I ever should see another such sight." In one letter to Mary, he implored her, "Pray for me." He reminded his brother, "I mean to do what is right as near as I can and let others do as they may." Unfortunately, William Silveus' experience ended in tragedy. Captured at the Battle of Fredericksburg on December 13, 1862, he contracted typhoid fever while confined in a Confederate prison. Eventually paroled, he reported to Camp Parole, Maryland, on January 9, 1863, and he died at the United States military hospital on the steamboat, "New York," on January 12, 1863.[29]

For the Greene County men who enlisted in Company A, 140th Pennsylvania Volunteers, it was Governor Curtin's call for twenty-one new volunteer regiments to serve for three years or the duration of the war which ignited their intent to enlist. Governor Curtin, responding to a call from President Lincoln for 300,000 more volunteers, had prefaced his call with a review of the Union disasters in the Peninsula Campaign in the summer of 1862 which brought the Confederate army of Northern Virginia "to the gates of Washington." At the time, James J. Purman was a student at Waynesburg College and a teacher at the school in Jacksonville, Richhill Township. He met with John F. McCullough from Jefferson, Pennsylvania, who had experience with the 1st Pennsylvania Cavalry, and David Taylor of Waynesburg at the "Hamilton House" in Waynesburg to discuss raising a company of cavalry. The three young men made an agreement to pursue the venture, and Purman began recruiting in Richhill, Centre, and Aleppo Townships in the western end of the county. He enrolled, first, James M. Pipes, and then John A. Burns, both of whom served eventually as captains of Company A. Years after the war, John

Burns' brother, James Burns, remembered how his family took the news about his enlistment:

> When the President's call was issued your father [John Burns] lacked one day of being nineteen years of age. At the time of the call he was a Freshman in Waynesburg College. Without consulting his father or mother he enlisted, packed his books and his clothing, and came home. How well I remember the day. I was a lad of eleven years. Father was plowing corn at the upper end of the farm and I was playing under a service tree. At ten o'clock the dinner horn blew. "Something is wrong at the house," said father; and, unhitching the horse, we went home. As we neared the house my mother, with restless step and tearful eye, came out to meet us. "John has enlisted," she said. Going into the house, we found him there with J. J. Purman, a fellow student, who had taught our district school the winter before. Securing horses from my father, they rode over the township, soliciting and urging other young men to enlist. They secured a dozen or more. . . . One summer morning about the last of July, these recruits assembled at our house to leave for the front. Many friends came with them. The parting was a sad one. I can see them even now, and feel the same swelling in the throat that I felt that July morning as I saw these men clamber into the two-horse wagons, father driving one of them, to be driven to Waynesburg. Here they were joined by eighty or ninety more men from other parts of the county.[30]

Upon hearing that the government was not taking any more cavalry regiments, the recruits designated themselves as the "Greene County Rifles," and offered themselves as an infantry company. When the 140th Regiment was formed, John F. McCullough was the Captain of Company A, J. J. Purman was First Lieutenant, and David Taylor served as Second Lieutenant.

A Union meeting was held at the Jollytown Methodist Church on August 24, 1861, attended by residents from Gilmore and the adjoining townships. "General" Spencer

Morris addressed the meeting "with a very patriotic speech." He told his listeners that "the real design" of the traitors in the South "was to destroy the Government of our Fathers and erect upon its ruins a strong Government or a limited Aristocracy." The speech concluded with "a scathing remark" about "rebel sympathizers in our own native hills of Greene county." "General" Morris declared himself for "bold forward war" against the enemies of the country. As the meeting ended, nineteen residents of Gilmore Township volunteered to serve in a company being raised by B. F. Morris.[31] At a union meeting in Mount Morris on September 6, 1861, J. A. J. Buchanan "withered" the "Secession proclivities, in this corner," with the power of his logic "in a highly eloquent and patriotic address."[32] In September 1861, twenty-one-year-old Joshua Rice decided to enlist in Captain James B. Morris' Company F, Seventh (West) Virginia Infantry, as he was working in the fields. He drove the team to the barn and unhitched, wiping the sweat from his face as he traveled to see the recruiters at the Jollytown Methodist Episcopal Church.[33] Another Jollytown area man, Henry Solomon White, that same month determined to enlist in "a company for the purpose of guarding bridges on the B&O R. R. for the term of 3 years or during the war if not sooner discharged."[34] On September 26, 1861, White's company was "escorted to Burton in wagons." He noted that "we stopped at Wareen [Warren] and cheered the citizens for some time and then went on to Burton hollowing like wolves." As the recruits made their way to be mustered into the Sixth (West) Virginia Infantry, White remembered, "we were a merry set of boys today sure."[35]

Isaac Scherich, another young man from western Greene County, had quite a different experience when he decided to enlist in the cause of the Union. Scherich's family lived on a farm in Richhill Township located on the border with the panhandle of western Virginia. Two hundred acres of the farm were located in Pennsylvania, along with the house, barn, and out buildings, and fifty-six acres were located in Virginia. He was five miles from Jacktown and eight miles from Cameron, Virginia. When Virginia seceded, Scherich joined a company being raised in Cameron and left for Wheeling. When the company was mustered in, however, the recruiting officer determined that he was too small at one hundred twenty pounds, and he was rejected from service in the army. Four more times he tried joining different companies being formed, and each time he was rejected. His father argued that he was too young, and the recruiting officers all believed he was too small for the hardships of army life. By the fall of 1862, Scherich had become discouraged:

> . . . so there I was. Could do nothing but work on the farm, at which I had been making a full hand for more than three years, at all kinds of work, such as plowing, mowing grass with a scythe, cutting grain with a cradle and raking 100 rails in a day, which was considered a good days work for a man; still I was too young and too small to be a soldier.[36]

Scherich finally got his chance to enlist after the family received a visit from Frank Campbell, a Waynesburg wool buyer with the firm of Campbell and Sons. Campbell told Scherich that his father had informed him about Scherich's desire to enlist. The elder Scherich said he thought his son was too young, but if he could get into the army, he would do nothing to get him out. Before leaving, Campbell told Isaac, ". . . whenever you want to enlist come to me and I will get you in." Early on the morning of September 9, 1862, Scherich "crawled out of bed . . . got out of the house as noiselessly as possible and started for Waynesburg, 24 miles away." Once in town, Campbell met the young man and took him straight to be enrolled in a company being formed for the Eighteenth Pennsylvania Cavalry. He also gave Scherich "a new hat to replace the one I had, which he said was not fit for a soldier to wear."[37]

Greene County boys continued to enlist as late as 1864. As an older man living in Bloomfield, Ohio, after the war, D. S. Hopkins remembered the exuberance of his youth:

> On the 26th of Feb 1864 at the age of 18 in company with 2 of my school mates John Simpson and Job Smith, we bid adieu to friends and loved ones, and left our homes at Hopkins Mills Greene Co Pa to enlist in the

A unique recruit from Greene County was a Mexican, Antonio Moralles. Moralles had been brought to Pennsylvania when he was about eleven years old. A private in the Duquesne Greys, Norton S. McGiffin, found Moralles in the town of Puebla near the close of the Mexican War. Taking the boy under his care, McGiffin brought him back to Washington, Pennsylvania, where he saw that the young lad attended school for two or three years and then apprenticed him to learn the blacksmithing trade. After completing his apprenticeship, Moralles set up a shop of his own in Greene County. He was quite successful in his business when the call for troops was made by President Lincoln. Moralles at that point determined to offer his services to his adopted country. Hearing that McGiffin was forming a volunteer company of infantry in Washington, Moralles sold his shop and hastened to Washington to enlist. Finding that McGiffin had already filled his company and left for Harrisburg, Moralles enlisted in a company of infantry being raised by Captain Alexander Wishart, Company K, 8th Pennsylvania Reserves. Moralles was mustered into Company K on June 22, 1861. He served throughout his three year enlistment, sharing in all the battles and hardships known by the men of the 8th Pennsylvania Reserves. Coming through it all unhurt, Moralles was mustered out with Company K on May 24, 1864. At that time, he returned to Greene County to continue his blacksmithing trade.[39]

"The fires of patriotism burn brightly in 'Little Greene,'" mused the *Messenger* in August 1861, "and she is standing up nobly for the flag and government of our fathers."[40] The county that summer had already provided three companies for the war effort, and it was estimated that four hundred Greene County men were serving with the national army. Aleppo Township in western Greene alone provided forty men to serve in loyal regiments in western Virginia. As the editors of the Democratic paper asked, "Who dare say, in view of these significant facts, that the people of this part of the State are failing or flagging in their duty?"[41] The *Waynesburg Messenger*, on September 4, 1861, further described a "Union Meeting" held in Waynesburg. The purpose of the meeting was the recruitment of a regiment for service in the war. Fayette County Democrat, "General" Joshua B. Howell, addressed the meeting, stating that Lincoln, as the duly elected President, "was entitled to the support of the people of all parties." He stated that partisanship should be put aside as long as "rebellion was rampant" in the country. The *Messenger* noted that Howell's remarks "frequently elicited applause." Greene County Democratic leaders also addressed the meeting, including J. A. J. Buchanan, James Lindsey, and Jesse Lazear. When the rally was over, the crowd "dispersed with three cheers for the Union, for General Howell, and Captain Gordon," whose local militia unit, The Pursley Guards, enrolled in Howell's new regiment, later designated the 85th Pennsylvania Volunteer Infantry.[42]

Patriotism continued running high the next summer, as the *Waynesburg Messenger* reported on July 16, 1862, when the women of the town were organizing a soldiers' relief society.[43] The leading women of Waynesburg met at Mrs. Jesse Lazear's house to form this new philanthropic group to help ease the suffering of wounded and sick soldiers in the field. As early as September 1861, Miss Mary A. Cooke had sought women in the county to knit socks and provide blankets for soldiers in the field.[44] On January 13, 1862, D. Stanton, regimental surgeon for the 1st Pennsylvania Cavalry, thanked the women of the Carmichaels Soldiers' Aid Society "for a most acceptable present—a large box of well selected clothing and bedding; quilts, blankets, socks, pillows, shirts, etc.; and all so good, warm, strong, substantial and comfortable." Stanton noted that much "good can be done, and has been done, by these Societies." The officers of the Carmichaels Society were listed as Miss Emily Cree, President, Miss Sarah Michener, Vice President, Miss Lide Hartman, Treasurer, and Miss Mell. Jamison, secretary.[45]

The Waynesburg Soldiers' Relief Society sought sheets, shirts, drawers, bandages, towels, canned and dried fruits, pickles, and jellies. An appeal was made to all "the patriotic ladies of the County." William A. Porter agreed to collect donated items at his store in Waynesburg.[46] Women actively involved with the society included Mrs. Frances Burbridge Lazear (Jesse Lazear's wife), Mrs. Benjamin Campbell, Mrs.

W. G. Scott, Miss Marcy C. Black, Miss Jennie Teagarden, Miss Haddie C. Miller, Mrs. M. Dill, Miss Mattie H. Parker, Mrs. Hannah Minor, and Mrs. Margaret Bell Miller, along with many others. The Waynesburg Soldiers' Relief Society gathered donations from all across the county, including hospital stores and a number of other articles from similar societies located on Muddy Creek and in Morris Township. By October 9, 1862, a Relief Association for sick and wounded soldiers had been formed in Jefferson, Pennsylvania, with D. L. Eaton as Chairman of the Finance Committee and Miss R. P. McCullough as corresponding secretary.[47] In addition to soliciting donations, the Waynesburg society also held occasional fund raising "festivals" at College Hall in Waynesburg with literary exercises and the sale of "sweetmeats." By October 8, 1862, the Waynesburg women had disbursed $158.97 for materials to make and send a supply of shirts, drawers, wrappers, pads, sheets, pillows, socks, and other assorted linens to Washington, D.C. In addition, the two large boxes sent to the nation's capital also included seventy cans of fruit, jellies, vinegar, and a large quantity of dried fruit. Also a box of groceries valued at twenty dollars, a barrel of onions, and a large box of clothing and linens were sent to St. Louis.[48] As Christmas approached in 1862, the *Waynesburg Messenger* reported that the "Ladies of Waynesburg are doing a good and patriotic work, through the Aid Society, for the gallant lads who have been wounded in battle or disabled by disease."[49]

Yet, there were still unsettling hints of problems that would emerge before the war ran its course. In 1861 there had been forty-five or fifty original members in the Ringgold Cavalry militia company. Of this number, all but nine or ten decided not to enlist when the unit was called for active duty, their places quickly being filled by other men eager to serve. One young man from Morgan Township, Greene County, however, who had declined active service with the Ringgold Cavalry, was "most shamefully abused and vilified." A correspondent to the *Waynesburg Messenger*, identified simply as "Fair Play," described the young man, Samuel Montgomery, as "intelligent and estimable." Reminding his readers that each individual who had decided against service was the best judge of his own conscience and sense of duty to his country, family, and himself, he protested "against singling out one or two individuals, and heaping odious epithets upon them for not going, while scores of others, in the same situation, are unmolested and permitted to pass without a word." He believed that the only reason Montgomery had been singled out for such treatment was the fact that he spoke his opinion regarding the cause of the war and openly regretted that an honorable compromise could not have been negotiated to prevent the disaster that now brought the horrors of civil war to the country.[50]

Nearly twenty years after the war, Reverend William Hanna reminded the readers of his history of Greene County that the ancestors of many county residents in the 1860s came from Virginia. For Hanna, therefore, it was "by no means strange that many" descendants of the county's pioneers "should have imbibed the notion of 'State Rights' . . . ."[51] From Lake Township in Mercer County, Pennsylvania, Anthony Silveus, brother of William Silveus of Centre Township in Greene County, who enlisted in Company I, 8th Pennsylvania Reserve Infantry, wrote to his brothers and sisters on October 8, 1862, looking for news from home and asking about "who of the old neighbors went to the war." With the Congressional elections approaching, it is evident that Anthony had additional motives for his letter. "Liberty," he said, "is all gone." Developing his point, the former Greene County man added:

> I do not know how my views will suit your politics or mind, but I think this trouble might all have been over if the negro lovers would not have had the power in our Congress. I believe that there might long before this time there might have been a compromise with the rebellious part of our country. I hope that you will all agree with me and cast your ballot in that way to prevent so much bloodshed and for peace and for the union as it was and the Constitution as it is . . . ."[52]

In Greene County, Abel Cary accused George Wisecarver of saying that he, Wisecarver, was "a Secessionist, and he didn't care a d---n who knew it." He also allegedly told Cary that there was no government and that Cary's son "had gone to support a pack of d----d Abolitionists." Wisecarver

31

denied the charge and countered that Cary had threatened "'shooting me' in daylight." The *Messenger* dismissed the subject as "a personal matter and of little interest to the general reader." Still, the paper recognized the charges as "unfortunate misunderstandings between neighbors and old friends."[53]

Greene County soldiers in Captain John Morris' company of the 85th Pennsylvania Volunteer Infantry held a meeting at Fort Good Hope near Washington, D. C., and passed a resolution, published in the *Greene County Republican,* condemning the Greene County Commissioners for failing to properly provide financial relief to their children and wives as promised by them under Pennsylvania state law at the time the men enlisted for military service. One hundred thirty soldiers endorsed a resolution which, among others, protested the Greene County Relief Board "arraigning our wives and mothers before the inquisitions, and compelling them to answer degrading, insulting, and humiliating questions, in order that they might receive the small portion that belongs to them by an act of the Legislature."[54] The law required that those claiming the relief complete an application providing basic family and financial information. "Two respectable citizens of the same neighborhood" were then required to certify the facts set forth in the claim application. The men of Captain Morris' company were further angered, and D. T. Ullom was threatened with "Judge Lynch," when it was rumored that he had stated that the new Poor Farm, approved by the county in 1861, would soon be finished in spring 1862 and that soldiers' wives and children could be taken care of there at little expense. Members of the county Relief Board and Ullom denied that any such conversations had occurred. The slander was attributed to party prejudice by Republicans and members of the county Board of Relief responded by stating that of relief supplied to soldiers' families from Greene County, nearly one-half had been furnished to families of men in Captain Morris' company of the 85th Infantry. The Relief Board noted, moreover, that families of county soldiers in (West) Virginia regiments were also entitled to relief if warranted.[55]

Despite assurances to the contrary, the problem with support for Greene County recruits' families had not been resolved by the autumn of 1862. J. J. Purman wrote a letter from Parkton, Maryland, on October 25, 1862. While relaying camp news and correcting an earlier publication in the *Waynesburg Messenger* regarding numbers of men in Company A, 140th Pennsylvania Volunteers, Lieutenant Purman commented on the number of married men in the company's total of one hundred two volunteers:

> The married men in our Company is 27; and, by the way, let me say, that these twenty-seven men think the Commissioners of Greene County are treating them and their wives and children very unjustly, in not fulfilling the promises made them to relieve the wants of their several families, whilst they are fighting to sustain our laws, our government, and our Union.[56]

Among the Greene County men serving in western Virginia regiments was Henry Solomon White, from the Jollytown area, who enlisted in Company N of the 6th (West) Virginia Infantry in September 1861, eventually serving as a corporal in the outfit. The 6th (West) Virginia was used primarily to guard the B&O Railroad facilities in western Virginia and spent most of its time on patrols looking for guerrilla bands, guarding railroad bridges, and fighting off raids by Confederate cavalry and infantry from eastern Virginia. White kept a small diary of his experiences, and an abstract of that diary is in the collection of the Cornerstone Genealogical Society. An outspoken supporter of the Union war effort, White noted in his diary, on April 15, 1862, that "bushwhackers have begun their guerrilla warfare in this country [near Fairmont] this spring. I hope they will meet with untimely graves. They must give over and quit their secession principles or their lives, either will do."[57]

Three weeks later, Captain J. H. Showalter of Company A received information that some of these "bushwhackers" had dispersed, agreeing to meet and reorganize at Davistown in Dunkard Township, Greene County, Pennsylvania. On Monday, May 5, 1862, therefore, White made an ominous entry in his diary regarding his native county. He wrote that Lieutenant Pierpont of Company A had come to the camp of

Company N to get some men to help "scout Monongalia, Greene, and Fayette Counties for secessionists and Knights of the Golden Circle [a secret organization of Southern sympathizers]." Leaving camp around four o'clock in the afternoon, the detachment of seventy men from companies A and N was accompanied by Captain Showalter and Lieutenant Pierpont of Company A, and Captain John Kenney and Lieutenant Jackson Moore of Company N. Marching at night, the men reached Laurel Point in Monongalia County, (West) Virginia, on Tuesday. After a day's rest, they set out for Davistown, eighteen miles away, that night. Crossing the border into Pennsylvania, the troop of Union soldiers stealthily approached the sleeping village, arriving on the outskirts of Davistown around three o'clock in the morning. Under cover of early morning darkness, Captain Showalter arranged his men on the ridges that enclosed the town.[58]

In an article published May 14, 1862, *The Waynesburg Messenger* reported that the "inhabitants of the little town were greatly astonished when they awoke up in the morning and found a picket of seventy soldiers armed with the unerring Minie rifle, stationed on the hills around the town." The Federal soldiers made a thorough search of the vicinity, but could not find any of the rebels they were hunting. White was not present, but in his diary on May 9, 1862, he noted that the "scouters" returned to camp and nothing much happened "while they were gone more than the inhabitants were very much frightened at the approach of our men in that country."[59]

Calling the incident "A Speck of War in Greene County," the correspondent for the *Messenger* added that the residents of Davistown "served up" a warm breakfast, "which was eagerly discussed by the wet and hungry soldiers." He further added that the "soldiers speak highly of the hospitality of the citizens of Davistown and vicinity."[60]

The first reported encounter between Greene County civilians and armed Federal troops during the Civil War ended, after some initial trepidation, in a public display of patriotism and hospitality. Reports of Knights of the Golden Circle operating in the area of Davistown appeared false. Whether future encounters would end so happily remained to be seen.

[1] G. Wayne Smith, *History of Greene County, Pennsylvania* (Waynesburg, Pennsylvania: Cornerstone Genealogical Society, 1996), p. 27.

[2] Evans, p. 167.

[3] *Pennsylvania Daily Telegraph* (Harrisburg), 1 May 1862, p. 2.

[4] "Pennsylvania Volunteers of the Civil War – Greene County Medal of Honor Recipients," http://www.pacivilwar.com/medalofhonor/greene.html, retrieved 9 March 2012.

[5] Smith, pp. 27-29.

[6] *Pennsylvania Daily Telegraph* (Harrisburg), 25 May 1861, p. 2.

[7] *Genius of Liberty* (Uniontown, PA), 30 May 1861, as quoted by Robert E. Eberly, Jr., *Bouquets from the Cannon's Mouth: Soldiering with the Eighth Regiment of the Pennsylvania Reserves* (Shippensburg, PA: White Mane Books, 2005), p. 14.

[8] *The Press* (Philadelphia, PA), 13 June 1861, p. 2.

[9] *Ibid.*

[10] *Genius of Liberty*, 30 May 1861 (as quoted by Eberly, p. 15).

[11] Samuel Clarke Farrar, *The Twenty-Second Pennsylvania Cavalry and the Ringgold Battalion, 1861-1865* (Pittsburgh: The New Werner Co., 1911), p. 12.

[12] Hanna, p. 323-324.

[13] *Ibid*, p. 324.

[14] Professor Robert Laird Stewart, D.D., *History of the One Hundred and Fortieth Regiment Pennsylvania Volunteers* (published by authority of the regimental association, 1912), p. 4.

[15] William Silveus to Mary Silveus, 19 September 1862, and William Silveus to Joe Silveus, postscript to letter to Mary Silveus, 20 September 1862 (private collection of D. Kent Fonner); also see D. Kent Fonner, "Dear Mary: The Civil War Letters of William Silveus," *Cornerstone Clues*, Vol. XX, #1 (February 1995), p. 18.

[16] *Waynesburg Messenger,* 30 July 1862, p. 3.

[17] *Ibid.* Also see *Waynesburg Messenger,* 6 August 1862, p. 2.

[18] *Ibid,* 13 August 1862, p. 2.

[19] *Ibid,* 20 August 1862, p. 3.

[20] *Ibid,* 20 August 1862, p. 3, and 27 August 1862, p. 3.

[21] *Ibid,* 4 February 1863, p. 3.

[22] *Ibid,* 15 April 1863, p. 2.

[23] *Republican Compiler* (Gettysburg), 19 January 1863, p. 2.

[24] *Pennsylvania Daily Telegraph* (Harrisburg), 20 August 1864, p. 2.

[25] *Waynesburg Messenger,* 2 December 1863, p. 3.

[26] *Ibid,* 3 February 1864, p. 3; 10 February 1864, p. 2.

[27] *Ibid,* 23 March 1864, p. 3.

[28] *Ibid,* 17 February 1864, p. 2.

[29] Letters of William Silveus are in the D. Kent Fonner collection. These were published by D. Kent Fonner, "Dear Mary: the Civil War Letters of William Silveus, Company I, 8th Pennsylvania Reserves," *Cornerstone Clues,* Vol. XX, No. 1 (February 1995), pp. 16-19.

[30] Stewart, pp. 5-6.

[31] *Waynesburg Messenger,* 11 September 1861, p. 2.

[32] *Waynesburg Messenger,* 26 September 1861, p. 2.

[33] Katherine O'Brien, *The Seventh West Virginia Volunteer Infantry* (Thesis submitted for M.A. in the Faculty of the Graduate School of West Virginia University: Morgantown, W. Va., 1965), p. 10.

[34] "Abstract from Diary Kept by Henry Solomon White in the Period Between September 1861 and June 1865," Manuscript Collection of the Cornerstone Genealogical Society, Waynesburg, PA, entry for 24 September 1861.

[35] *Ibid*, 26 September 1861.

[36] "The 18th Pennsylvania Rides Again!!," a transcription of the memoirs/journal of Private Isaac Scherich, Company A, 18th Pennsylvania Cavalry (available at the Cornerstone Genealogical Society, Waynesburg, Pa.), p. 1.

The original of Isaac Scherich's journal is in the Trans-Appalachian Room of the Waynesburg University Library, Waynesburg, PA.

[37] *Ibid*, pp. 1-2.

[38] D. S. Hopkins, "Reminiscence of My Service in the U. S. Army from 26th Day of February 1864 to 11th Day of July 1865," handwritten manuscript, PA Historical & Museum Commission, Division of Archives and Manuscripts, MG-6-Diaries and Journals-Box #1, p. 1.

[39] *Waynesburg Messenger*, 16 August 1865, p. 3.

[40] *Waynesburg Messenger,* 28 August 1861, p. 3.

[41] *Ibid.*

[42] *The Waynesburg Messenger*, 4 September 1861, as quoted by Andrew J. Waychoff, *Local History of Greene County and Southwestern Pennsylvania*, pp. 85-86. Other Greene County militia units incorporated in the 85th Pennsylvania included the Ten Mile Greys from Rogersville, the Waynesburg Invincibles, and the Monongahela Guards from Greensboro and Smithfield. See Luther S. Dickey, *History of the Eighty-fifth Regiment Pennsylvania Volunteer Infantry, 1861-1865* (New York, 1915), p. 6.

[43] *The Waynesburg Messenger*, Waynesburg, PA, 16 July 1862, p. 3.

[44] *Ibid,* 26 September 1861, p. 3.

[45] *Ibid,* 12 February 1862, p. 3.

[46] *Ibid,* 16 July 1862, p. 3.

[47] *Ibid,* 15 October 1862, p. 2.

[48] *Ibid.*

[49] *Ibid,* 24 December 1862, p. 3.

[50] *Waynesburg Messenger*, 11 September 1861, p. 2.

[51] Rev. William Hanna, *History of Greene County, PA*, p. 322.

[52] Anthony Silveus to his Brothers and Sisters, 8 October 1862, private collection of D. Kent Fonner, Beach Lake, Pennsylvania.

[53] *Waynesburg Messenger,* 22 October 1862, p. 2, and 14 January 1863, p. 3.

[54] *Waynesburg Messenger,* 2 April 1862, p. 2.

[55]*Ibid,* 2 April 1862, p. 2; 9 April 1862, p. 3. For a sample of the relief application see *Waynesburg Messenger*, 23 October 1861, p. 3.

[56] *Waynesburg Messenger,* 5 November 1862, p. 2.

[57]Henry Solomon White Diary, 15 April 1862.

[58] Henry Solomon White Diary, 5 May 1862. *Waynesburg Messenger*, 14 May 1862, p. 3.

[59] *Waynesburg Messenger*, 14 May 1862. Henry Solomon White Diary, 9 May 1862.

[60] *Waynesburg Messenger*, 14 May 1862, p. 3.

Home Front Vignette: "Our national anniversary . . ."

[*Greene County patriotism was evident in many local communities on July 4, 1862. The Waynesburg Messenger, in its issue published July 16, 1862, described "the most pleasant and interesting Celebrations."*]

"Our national anniversary was very generally celebrated throughout the county.

At Nineveh by the military and several Sabbath schools, our friend General Morris addressing them in an able and patriotic speech.

At the Baptist Church, on Pursley, where our bachelor neighbor, R. A. McConnell, Esq., made an exceedingly happy and appropriate speech, as we are informed.

At Carmichaels, by a 'large gathering,' which was addressed by J. A. J. Buchanan, Esq., in his usual eloquent and impressive manner.

At the Union Meeting House in Franklin Township, where President Miller delivered an address of great interest and profit to young and old.

And last, though not least, at the Ruff's Creek Baptist Church, by some six or eight Sabbath schools and a large concourse of citizens. The number participating was variously estimated at from 1500 to 2000. It was our good fortune to be present on the occasion, and we are free to say it was one of the most pleasant and interesting celebrations of the kind we have ever attended. Bountiful provision had been made for the outward man, and when all were 'filled,' almost enough remained to make a feast for a half thousand adults. – Professor

Black, of Washington College, addressed the Sabbath school children in one of the best juvenile speeches we have ever had the pleasure of listening to, while the oration was pronounced by A. A. Purman, Esq. of Waynesburg. As the audience, with hearty and perfect unanimity requested a copy of the address for publication, and as it will likely appear in our next paper, it is necessary to say but little of its merits. We must be permitted to remark, however, that it is a production of decided ability, bold and outspoken in its devotion to the great principles of constitutional liberty, and was heard with marked attention by an approving and appreciative audience."

Chapter III: "A Loyal Opposition"

As noted by Dr. G. Wayne Smith, "One constant in Greene County politics from the beginning was an affiliation with and unqualified support for the Democratic Party . . . ."[1] From the rise of the Jacksonian Democrats in the 1824 Presidential election down to 1860, and beyond, the county consistently voted for the party candidates. In 1844, the voters of Greene County supported Democrat James K. Polk with 2,354 votes, a majority of 1,932 votes out of 3,790 votes cast.[2] The people strongly supported President Polk's war against Mexico in 1846, and a Democrat party meeting at the Court House in Waynesburg in 1847 passed a resolution stating that "all those who are opposing the present war, and endeavoring to throw obstructions in the way of the government, are opposing the cause of justice and the country, and are giving encouragement to the enemy."[3]   After the state elections in October 1848, it was reported that the citizens of "Little Greene" have "the name of being the best of Democrats in the State."[4]   During the 1852 election campaign, the Pittsburgh *Daily Morning Post* rejoiced over "little Greene forever." "She is always sure," wrote the editor, "and will give a large democratic majority."[5] The importance of Greene County as a Democrat party base is reflected in the fact that during the 1850s, several county politicians held state offices, including Charles A. Black as Secretary of the Commonwealth in 1853 and Maxwell McCaslin who served six years as a state senator, twice serving as Speaker of the Pennsylvania Senate.

As the national Whig Party rapidly disintegrated over the slavery issue following the Mexican War and the national conflict surrounding the Kansas-Nebraska Act of 1854, the Know-Nothing Movement, or the American Party, made a brief showing in Greene County. The Know-Nothings advocated anti-foreign and anti-Catholic views. When asked about their organization's policies or activities, members responded, "I know nothing." The movement supported only native-born Americans (i.e. White, Protestant, males) to hold public offices. When Pennsylvania's Grand State Council of the Know-Nothings met in Pittsburgh in 1854, it was reported that the

Greene County lodges had seventeen hundred members. Although the state organization contained some Democrats, it was stated that a large majority of the order were Whigs. Despite the large number of members in Greene County, it was believed by the state leadership that the area was one of five counties in Pennsylvania where revelations about the nature of the Know-Nothing movement had been thoroughly circulated and that these counties would present the most danger to growth of the state movement.[6]

The prediction proved correct. Many Democrats abandoned the Know-Nothings as soon as they realized that members were being forced to oppose Democrat candidates for office and support candidates endorsed by Know-Nothing leaders. Less than a year later, thirteen well-known citizens of Richhill Township published a notice renouncing the Know-Nothings and stating the reasons that had induced them to originally give the movement their support. The men had joined because they believed that the movement was designed to "place some limitation upon the influence of our foreign population, as well as the Roman Catholics." They ashamedly admitted that they had failed to consider the injustice their opinions would impose on a large segment of the country's population. Feeling "grossly deceived" by the leaders of the organization, they were now convinced that the true goal of the movement was to place its leaders in power. As they claimed:

> Many of us were induced to enter the order on the representation that its objects were political, not intended to operate against the *true* principal [sic] of the Democratic party. We were surprised to hear, almost as soon as we entered, a project discussed, the side object and aim of which was to disorganize and break down the Democratic party. We therefore felt that a fraud has been practiced upon us, that relieved us from any supposed obligation we had taken.[7]

Greene County political leaders of both the Democrat and Whig parties continued to distance themselves from the Know-Nothings. The Know-Nothings nominated a full slate of candidates for the 1855 election. In Greene County, they nominated John E. Taylor for Assembly, Isaac Mitchell for Sheriff, Armstrong Grim for Commissioner, Alfred Myers for Treasurer, John H. Wells for District Attorney, and Job Throckmorton for Auditor. Mitchell, Wells, and Throckmorton all refused to accept their nominations.[8] By the summer of 1857, former state senator, John C. Flenniken, renounced both "Republicanism" and "Know-Nothingism," announcing that he would support Democrat President James Buchanan and "the Union."[9]

As the national crisis over Kansas-Nebraska grew in the last half of the 1850s, the rift in the Democratic party in the North between Douglas Democrats, supporters of Illinois Senator Stephan A. Douglas, and Buchanan Democrats could be seen in the career of Greene County Democrat state senator Maxwell McCaslin. Douglas' Kansas-Nebraska Act, organizing the territories of Kansas and Nebraska, in 1854, had provided that the issue of slavery in the newly created territories was to be decided by the residents themselves through the process of voting, the concept of "popular sovereignty." Passage of the law, however, led to armed conflict within Kansas territory over the issue of slavery. "Border Ruffians" from the neighboring slave state of Misssouri sought to influence settlement in the territory and subsequent elections in behalf of the cause of pro-slavery. They were met by a flood of anti-slavery settlers, especially from New England aided by the New England Emigrant Aid Society. Abolitionists in Boston sent arms to their Kansas settlers in boxes shipped as "Bibles," and the area soon became famous as "Bleeding Kansas," giving vent to such radicals as abolitionist John Brown and the pro-slavery United States Senator from Missouri, David Atchison. Pro-slavery forces in Kansas eventually elected a territorial legislature, which met in the town of Lecompton. Free state supporters refused to recognize the Lecompton government and formed their own territorial legislature in Topeka. By 1857, the pro-slavery government was seeking admission as a state under the proposed Lecompton state constitution, which included a strong provision protecting slaveholders' "property" and specifically excluding free blacks from its bill of rights. Voters in Kansas had not been given the opportunity to vote on the whole constitution, being limited to vote for the constitution with or without slavery. Free-staters, viewing the referendum as a farce, refused to vote, and so the Lecompton Constitution passed and was sent to Congress for approval. Douglas recognized that the Lecompton document was not the product of true popular sovereignty, and he opposed admission of Kansas as a state under its provisions. President Buchanan, on the other hand, seeking an end to the Kansas controversy, sought to use his power to force recognition of the proposed Lecompton state government.

In Greene County, Maxwell McCaslin, recognized as a "thorough-going Democrat," was a leader of the party and served in the Pennsylvania legislature for ten years, including six years as a state senator representing the Greene County district. McCaslin had been born in Martinsburg, Virginia, but by the 1850s had a Pennsylvania state-wide reputation as "one of the most talented and honored representatives ever sent from Democratic Greene." He was twice elected speaker of the Pennsylvania senate in 1850 and 1853. President Franklin Pierce appointed McCaslin to be Indian Agent for the Osage River Agency in Kansas in March 1855. As soon as he reached the troubled territory, McCaslin's "rugged and honest" character brought him into opposition with the Missouri border ruffians and their attempt to sway public opinion and elections in Kansas by intimidation and violence. In 1858, he supported Buchanan's new territorial governor, Robert J. Walker, who quickly exposed the election frauds in the territory and rejected the Lecompton returns. McCaslin wrote to his friends in Pennsylvania, in March 1858, urging them not to support the Lecompton Constitution or "lend themselves to aiding this wrong." The letter, in the possession of Greene County assemblyman William Kincaid, argued "that the army of the United States, multiplied by ten, could not for a single month enforce the Lecompton Constitution upon the people of Kansas, so repugnant as it is in itself, and such a stench in their nostrils are its authors." Buchanan summarily dismissed Governor Walker from his office, and McCaslin, before the end of the month, was also removed from his position as Indian Agent. He returned east and then retired to a farm he had purchased near Parkersburg, Virginia. When the civil war erupted, although "advanced in years," McCaslin determined to offer himself in defense of the country; and he formed a regiment, the 15th (West) Virginia Infantry, which he commanded for two years until he resigned due to ill health.[10]

After 1856, even the opposition party in Greene County, the Republican, sometimes divided over the Lecompton issue, with a faction of party members supporting Democratic candidates. On January 3, 1859, William H. Wells, the oldest son of John H. Wells, a respected Waynesburg lawyer and notary public, drafted a letter to the nationally-famous Illinois lawyer and politician, Abraham Lincoln. Wells' father was noted as an outspoken supporter of the Whig, and later, the Republican parties in Greene County before the Civil War. John H. Wells had even been elected during the antebellum period to serve for a time as commander of the state militia brigade that included the Greene County units. In 1852, the leaders of the Whig Party induced "General" Wells to take charge of the *Greene County Whig*, the newspaper that later was known as the *Greene County Republican*.[11] William H. Wells told Lincoln that his father "devoted more time and money to the Whig party in its day, & to the Republican Party in *its* day, than any man in our County." Describing himself as "a young man, & only a 'jour printer,'" Wells enclosed with his letter to Lincoln an undated clipping from the *Waynesburg Messenger* containing a letter describing his dispute with Mr. E. R. Bartleson, editor of the *Greene County Republican* at the time. Wells alleged in his letter to the *Messenger* that Bartleson had been "a source of mortification and damage to the Republican party." Claiming that Bartleson failed to support any Republican candidates, despite his position as editor of the county's only Republican newspaper, Wells noted that Bartleson was supporting Stephen A. Douglas and other "anti-Lecompte" Democrats for national and state offices. Apparently, in the 1858 Congressional elections, according to the younger Wells, Bartleson supported the Democratic candidate, William Montgomery, although he had promised to back the election of Republican Jonathon Knight. Feeling that the party was betrayed, Wells called on other Greene County Republicans to "reflect calmly on this matter." "Our *'organ'* has betrayed us once," he wrote, "let us guard against treachery in the future."[12] Seeking material from Lincoln's famous

45

debates with Douglas to support his battle with Bartleson, Wells told Lincoln, ". . . I would be greatly obliged if you would send me the speech delivered, I think, at Freeport, in which the Dred Scott decision & 'popular sovereignty' are discussed."[13]

Abraham Lincoln responded to Mr. Wells' letter on January 8, 1859. He told the young Waynesburg Republican that his debates with Douglas had not been published except in the newspapers. At that time, Lincoln, regretfully, had no copies to send Wells. He was in the process of gathering a single set of newspaper reports for himself, and he promised to keep Wells' address and send him a copy of the "Freeport discussion" if he could find an old newspaper "in a reasonable time." As to the issue of Republicans supporting Douglas and Douglas Democrats for political office, Lincoln viewed such "dallying" as "at the very least, time, and labor lost . . . ." He believed Douglas' policies regarding slavery would eventually lead to "the nationalization of this institution." So long as Douglas supported the Supreme Court's decision in the Dred Scott case and advocated "popular sovereignty," caring "not whether slavery be voted down or voted up; that it is simply a question of dollars and cents, and that the Almighty has drawn a line on one side of which labor must be performed by slaves; to support him or Buchanan, is simply to reach the same goal by only slightly different roads."[14]

When the war started in 1861, William H. Wells was residing in Missouri. After Lincoln's initial call for volunteers, following the attack on Fort Sumter, Wells joined Captain Cole's Company E, First Regiment Missouri Volunteers, organized in St. Louis. Wells and the First Missouri fought in the battles at Boonville, Dug Springs, and Springfield, Missouri. At Springfield, in the Battle of Wilson's Creek, the Union army, under the command of Brigadier General Nathaniel Lyon, engaged in a severe fight that cost the lives of General Lyon and over two thousand Federal soldiers. The First Missouri opened the battle, and Wells wrote to his mother that he was "in the thickest of the fight, and you may rest assured I tried to do my duty as a soldier." Company E lost twenty-eight out of sixty-five men, "but through the providence of God" Wells "escaped unharmed."[15] In December 1861, Wells made a visit to Greene County after being discharged from the First Missouri. He worked for a while as foreman of the *Waynesburg Messenger* print shop until it was announced he had received an appointment from Pennsylvania Governor Andrew Curtin as a First Lieutenant in Colonel Coulter's regiment of the Pennsylvania Reserve Corps. His bosses at the *Messenger* wrote that they rejoiced "most sincerely in the tardy justice done our gallant young friend, 'by the powers that be,' for his bravery and good conduct in last Summer's campaign in Missouri."[16]

Republican Party members were a rarity in Greene County politics in the 1860s. At the township elections in the spring of 1862, only seventeen Republican candidates were elected out of a total of eighty-three township offices.[17] When Republican Party leaders called a meeting at the Court House in June 1862, the *Waynesburg Messenger* reported the attendance as a "small gathering of the 'faithful few' who still cling to the fortunes of this doomed, if not already obsolete party." Only fifteen or twenty "full-grown, bearded adults participated" when a vote was taken during the course of the meeting.[18] The Republican County Convention in late summer 1862 was attended by only twelve delegates.[19] The 1863 county convention had to adjourn for lack of a quorum. When the convention finally met in late August, the Democrat newspaper joked that by "dint of great effort, and by pressing a number of farmers into service who came to town on different and better paying and more reputable business, the Government hirelings and pensioners here at Waynesburg succeeded in 'counting noses' from sixteen of the twenty-one districts." It was also noted that several townships were only represented by one delegate, and "in most instances he looked ashamed of himself." Nominations made for county and state offices included Zadock Gordon of Centre Township for state assembly, John Remley, of Centre Township for county treasurer, Joshua Ackley of Richhill Township for county commissioner, John Smith of Morgan Township for auditor, and Josephus H. Morris of Greene Township for poor house director.[20] The entire Republican slate for county offices was defeated in the general election that year. Republican Party patronage supplied Zadock Gordon with a local position in the spring when the Lincoln administration removed Democrat Abram Kent from his position as post master at Oak Forest and appointed Gordon to fill the vacancy.[21]   In January 1865, party politics again expressed itself in the post office administration when a decision was made by Lincoln's postmaster general to abolish the Davidson Ferry Post Office. Joseph G. Garrard observed, "It is a little too Democratic about Davidson's Ferry to please Uncle Abe's friends about the river."[22]

In 1860, Democrat-controlled Greene County voted against Lincoln. That year, in Illinois, a future leader of the county's Republican Party, Waynesburg College graduate J. B. Donley, Congressman from Greene County in 1869 and future son-in-law of John H. Wells, cast his first ballot for President for Lincoln.[23]   Of 4,322 votes cast in Greene County in November, the southern Democrat candidate for President, John C. Breckinridge, Vice President of the United States under President Buchanan, and later serving as Senator from Kentucky, received 2,665 votes, while Lincoln received the second highest tally at 1,614 votes. Stephen A. Douglas, the northern Democrat candidate only received twenty-six votes. In 1864, Greene County was one of twelve counties in the state of Pennsylvania that voted against Lincoln's reelection.   The county gave Democrat George B. McClellan 3,074 votes out of 4,657 votes cast.[24]

As early in the secession crisis as February 16, 1861, with the country drifting toward open hostilities between states of the lower South and the Federal government, Greene County Democrats held a meeting at the Courthouse in Waynesburg to pick delegates to send to Harrisburg for a convention calling for peace and supporting compromise with the South. Charles A. Black, Congressman Jesse Lazear, J. L. McConnell, and Dr. S. Morris were selected as delegates. In his diary that evening, James Lindsey, law partner of J.A.J. Buchanan, Chairman of the County Democratic Committee, wrote that he gave an hour-long speech supporting the resolution for a compromise with the seceding states. He stated that if Lincoln and the Republicans "stubbornly reject all compromises, and recklessly plunge the country into Civil War, they would have to do the fighting themselves." His remarks were met with great applause by the assembly and, to him, "seemed to embody the unanimous sentiment of the meeting."[25]

Lindsey, born on November 21, 1827, was the eldest child of a long-time Greene County Democrat leader, John Lindsey, who had served one term as sheriff (1846-1849) and two terms as prothonotary and clerk of courts (1851-1857). Educated at the Greene Academy in Carmichaels, James Lindsey was admitted to the practice of law in 1852. Like his father, he soon took an active role in local politics. At a Greene County Democrat meeting on December 15, 1856, the young Lindsey was appointed the county delegate to the Democrat state convention that met in Harrisburg on March 2, 1857, to choose William F. Packer the state party candidate for governor that year.[26] Lindsey's diary, in the winter of 1861, reveals something of the struggle that the leaders of Greene County experienced about their own loyalties as war approached. On January 2, 1861, he noticed that the "signs of the times are very dark and portentous." He believed that "the Union ought, if possible, to be preserved, at all hazards and at every cost."[27] On Friday, January 4, 1861, Lindsey and his wife, Sarah, the daughter of Dr. Arthur Inghram, attended a religious service in the morning at the Greene County Courthouse held in celebration of a day of fasting and prayer called by President Buchanan for the whole country. The young attorney was not satisfied with the response:

> The attendance was painfully slim. I fear it is evidence that few of the citizens of Waynesburg are accustomed to implore Divine Assistance in time of danger. Certainly they are either ignorant of the perils now impending over our beloved country, or reckless of the consequences. Rev'd mr Ewing of the Presbyterian Church delivered a sensible and conservative Address.

The Lindseys did not return to Waynesburg for the evening service, but their hired man and girl reported that "attendance was respectable."[28] The next day, Major John Gordon, commander of the Pursley Guards, dropped by Lindsey's office. The two men had a long conversation about political affairs. From their conversation, Lindsey reported "no signs of good omen; and a fear of Civil War is beginning to prevail." In his diary, he asked, "Can it be that we are drifting into the horrors of a French Revolution? May God, in his mercy, avert such a fate."[29]

By February 4, 1861, he believed that the "newspapers bring us news, which is only more and more alarming, respecting the critical condition of the Country." "In the Southern states," he thought, "madness seems to rule the hour." As to the Northern states, Lindsey was convinced that "the dominant political party [the Republican Party] seems intent only on party triumph." Since neither side seemed willing to find ground for compromise, he was convinced that if "the country is to be saved, the *people,* and not the politicians, will do it."[30] As for Abraham Lincoln, after reading his inaugural address in the *Pittsburgh Evening Chronicle*, Lindsey believed "he is not the man for the Crisis." From his perusal of the speech, Lindsey was certain that Lincoln "seems incapable of rising far enough above the *Partizan* to meet the great questions of the day, in the true and lofty spirit of *patriotism. "* Lindsey believed that Lincoln lacked the moral courage to resist the radical wing of the Republican Party and that his policies would "precipitate war" and "drive off the border Slave States." Still, Lindsey saw him as the constitutionally elected President, and he was willing to see him supported if he adopted "a wise, conciliatory and patriotic policy."[31]

In October 1861, the thirty-three-year-old Waynesburg attorney was elected President Judge of the Fourteenth Judicial District, including the courts of Greene, Washington, and Fayette Counties. The *Waynesburg Messenger* proudly proclaimed that Lindsey "made a fine run," with a "thundering majority" of at least twenty-two hundred votes over his opponent, Republican James Veech of Fayette County.[32] During the campaign, a Fayette County Republican newspaper tried to dismiss Lindsey as a "small fry politician" who gave speeches condemning President Abraham Lincoln for violating the Constitution in his attempt to put down the southern rebellion but who made no condemnation of the leaders of that rebellion like Jefferson Davis. The *Messenger* responded that Lindsey "is not a neutral man, his opinions are well-known, and his patriotism and loyalty have never been doubted." Lindsey viewed the war as a "death struggle for Constitutional Liberty and Law." "In his opinion," noted his supporters, "the Union and Government are worth any sacrifice that their perpetuation may demand."[33] Democrats in Greene County knew Lindsey as "a courteous gentleman in business and social intercourse, and endowed with an intellect of rare quickness and vigor." It was expected that James Lindsey would make "an able and popular judge."[34]

On August 7, 1862, Judge Lindsey summarized his matured opinion about the necessity of supporting the North's war effort in a letter to be read at a Washington County "War Meeting:"

> While the fate of our country hangs trembling in the balance, as it does this day, no true patriot should be silent, or inactive. Every motive which can influence noble natures should now inspire our efforts. Honor and duty; love of country and love of liberty; veneration for the government of our fathers; and solicitude for the interests of our posterity; safety for ourselves, secured by our nationality, and hope for the downtrodden of other lands; dread of the weakness which must, and the anarchy that may, follow a separation of these States; and apprehension of a yet greater revolution which may sprinkle every man's door-post with blood—these, and a hundred other motives, call upon us now, with trumpet tongue, to rally around the *old flag* and to strike valiantly for the Union and the Constitution.[35]

As war erupted between the two sections of the country, North and South, however, and with hundreds of Greene County men flocking to join the colors of the Union, the leaders of the Peace Democrats in the county remained steadfast in their opposition to many of the policies adopted by Lincoln and the Republican majority in Congress for prosecution of the war. To meet the crisis of Civil War, Lincoln suspended the use of the writ of habeas corpus, martial law was imposed even in some areas of the North on occasion when deemed necessary for the war effort, and military courts were used to try civilians charged with being in violation of military policies. As the war continued, Lincoln adopted a more radical policy by issuing the Emancipation Proclamation to take effect on January 1, 1863.

The Republican-controlled Congress enacted a most unpopular measure, on March 3, 1863, when it passed a military conscription act that allowed a man drafted into military service to hire a "substitute" or pay $300 to be exempted from service. As war weariness grew in the North, this draft law led to increasing charges that the conflict was a "rich man's war" but "a poor man's fight." Moreover, many Peace Democrats in the North saw the Emancipation Proclamation as unconstitutional and a stumbling block to any negotiated peace and reunion with the South.[36]

In Congress, Jesse Lazear, the son of Thomas Lazear from Richhill Township, was a stubborn opponent to the Republicans. Born on December 12, 1804, Congressman Lazear received limited schooling but like many in his generation became a "self-made man." He started his career as a teacher. His father having served as a magistrate in Richhill Township for many years, it was not long, however, before the young man became engaged in politics and local business ventures. He was elected Register of Wills and Recorder of Deeds for Greene County, serving in those offices from 1829 to 1832. He also was employed as the Cashier of the Farmers and Drovers Bank in Waynesburg much of his adult life from 1835 until 1867.[37] Lazear made a run for election to Congress to represent Greene, Fayette, and Washington counties in the Twentieth District of Pennsylvania in 1858. At that time he was opposed in the Democratic caucuses by William Montgomery. Lazear lost "after a warfare for the nomination, which we have never seen equalled [sic] in the State."[38] While there was some talk about challenging the nomination of Montgomery, Lazear, demonstrating Democratic Party loyalty, circulated a letter expressing that he could not "consent that my name should be used in opposition to the expressed will of a majority of the Democratic party of the District."[39] The gratification of party leaders for Lazear's actions was expressed by a resolution conceding "to Greene County the right to the nominee for Congress in 1860."[40] Accordingly, Jesse Lazear was nominated by the Democratic Party and was elected to represent the Twentieth District of Pennsylvania in Congress in the 1860 elections. Lazear served two terms in Congress as Greene County's representative in the Thirty-Seventh and the Thirty-

Eighth Congresses (1861-1865). In the Thirty-Eighth Congress, Lazear was elected to represent the newly-created Twenty-fourth District, including Greene, Washington, Beaver, and Lawrence Counties.

The *Waynesburg Messenger* explained Lazear's opposition to the Lincoln administration's conduct of the war:

> In a letter to the "Messenger" under date of Washington City, July 4th, after distinctly expressing the conviction that it was the "duty of Congress to sustain freely the administration in its just and loyal efforts to resist and crush out the rebellion," and after disavowing any wish, "much as he desired peace," to "offer any compromise to the rebels against the country," believing "they deserved the severest penalties of the law," General Lazear suggests the propriety of the present Congress taking the initiative in measures which guarantee to the South what he believes to be their constitutional right – that "of occupying the Territories on equal terms with the North." This he thinks due to the loyal states of Kentucky, Maryland, Delaware, and Missouri, as well as to the loyal people of the seceded States, and would, in his opinion, leave the rebels without pretext or apology for resisting the Government or seeking a dissolution of the Union.[41]

Lazear's policy with regard to the successful conclusion to the war was to seek a compromise that would bring the rebellious states back into the Union. General Lazear, however, was "no stickler for any particular mode of settling our difficulties." He favored the "Crittenden Compromise," as "being less likely to lead to mischievous and violent controversies on the subject of slavery where Territories are left open to either slave or free institutions." The *Messenger* found "much plausibility in this suggestion," and believed that "it will have its weight when this vexatious matter is finally disposed of, as it will be when the people assert their prerogative and ignore fanatical and dangerous politicians, with their dogmas and heresies."[42]

It was reported that Lazear was not a "noisy member" of Congress, but the Greene County Democrats believed him to be "one of the most industrious, able, and faithful" legislators "in the House." For a great many voters in Greene County, Congressman Lazear was "a great favorite . . . as well on account of his private virtues and fine social qualities, as because of his consistent and unswerving devotion to the interests of his country and his party." During the 1862 Congressional election campaign, he was lauded as a "man who thinks for himself, and speaks and votes his sentiments on all occasions, unawed by power and influence, and fearless of his foes." Lazear certainly represented the political view of a majority of Greene County residents. "The people here at home, who know him," reported the *Messenger* after his reelection to Congress in 1862, "have approved and endorsed his course and opinions with a degree of unanimity rarely met with at popular elections."[43]

On July 9, 1861, Freshman Congressman Lazear voted against a resolution passed by the House which absolved Union soldiers of any duty to capture and return escaped slaves.[44] Later that year, on December 10, 1861, Lazear supported a resolution, subsequently tabled by the House without action, stating that Congress alone had the right to suspend habeas corpus and that suspension of the writ by any other government department "is a usurpation and therefore dangerous to the liberty of the people."[45] On February 28, 1863, Lazear gave a speech before the House in which he defended his "pacific views", at the same time protesting against being abused and called "disloyal" for holding such views. "I confess that I would prefer a peace," he said, "rather than to have the people of the South exterminated . . . and to see their lands occupied by their discharged slaves, even if we were sure that they would raise no more cotton." In addition, he argued "that the arrests of citizens by military or executive authority are unconstitutional, and that whoever commits such an act of outrage is liable to an action for damages in our courts, from which responsibility no government power can shield him." For Lazear, martial law could "only exist where the will of the despot is supreme." As for the Emancipation Proclamation, he dismissed it as a measure "pregnant with more evil than any single act done by one man."[46] As late in the war as May 31, 1864, Congressman Lazear introduced a resolution that the President suspend all hostilities and call for a convention of delegates from all the states, North and South, to meet for the purpose of working out a compromise to end the war and to restore the southern states to the Union.[47] He opposed the passage of an amendment to the Constitution for the total abolition of slavery.[48] One Republican newspaper, *The Pennsylvania Daily Telegraph*, from Harrisburg, summed up many views expressed by Lincoln supporters, when the editor stated that the Twenty-Fourth Congressional District "is at present represented by Jesse Lazear, a rank copperhead."[49]

In the 1862 congressional election for the newly-created Twenty-fourth Congressional District in western Pennsylvania, Lazear was opposed by Republican, Dr. John W. Wallace of New Castle, Pennsylvania, running on the "Union" ticket, an alliance of Republicans and War Democrats.[50] Dr. Wallace had represented Lawrence County and the old Twenty-third Congressional District in the 37th Congress. An old line Whig with a reputation for conservatism, Dr. Wallace had been opposed for election to Congress in 1860 by the radical Republicans of his district. As a Congressman, however, Dr. Wallace had proven to be a strong ally of the Lincoln administration. Dr. Wallace joined radical Republicans like Thadeus Stevens from Pennsylvania in voting against a resolution reaffirming the Crittenden Compromise in late 1861. He supported the Confiscation Act of 1862 which provided that slaves escaping into Union lines were considered captives of war who were to be set free. Supporting Lincoln's various schemes for emancipation, such as the purchase of slaves by the government, Dr. Wallace had voted in favor of a resolution declaring the President's authority to free all the slaves in the rebel states under his authority as Commander-in-Chief. He voted in favor of emancipation of all slaves held in the District of Columbia. In a controversial vote in July 1862, Dr. Wallace supported a bill providing the President, in his discretion, the authority to enlist Blacks in the army and navy, and providing freedom for the mother, wife, and children of any "person of African descent" who enlisted. As election day approached, the *Waynesburg Messenger* reminded its readers:

Let the people bear in mind that in voting for Dr.

Wallace, they are voting for an OUT AND OUT ABOLITIONIST, *who is in favor of buying the Southern Slaves, at a cost of more than a* THOUSAND MILLIONS OF DOLLARS, and setting them at liberty to overrun the Northern States, and come into competition with the laboring classes here, and to fill our jails, penitentiaries and poor houses, at the expense of our already over-taxed people.[51]

Lazear won the general election on October 14, 1862, by a slim margin of 426 votes, including a majority vote in Greene County of more than two thousand. Wallace gave immediate notice that he was contesting the election. He claimed a majority of the votes legally cast in the twenty-fourth district, including "the soldiers' vote," which the return judges of the various counties in the district refused to count. In addition, Wallace alleged several other irregularities in the Greene County vote: 1) votes for Lazear in Dunkard Township and several other townships in Greene County cast by aliens; 2) votes in Wayne Township cast by persons under twenty-one years old; 3) votes cast in Richhill Township by citizens of Virginia; 4) persons allowed to vote in Marion Township who were not "white male citizens of the United States;" and 5) that elections in Franklin Township and other townships were held at illegal polling places.[52]

Democratic newspapers called Wallace's charges a "bold attempt at fraud." "We see it stated in the Abolition papers," wrote the editor of the *Greensburg Democrat*, as quoted in the *Lancaster Intelligencer*, "that a bogus army vote will be gotten up to deprive . . . Jesse Lazear" of his seat. "We register our solemn determination," he continued, "to resist the consummation of this fraud even unto blood."[53] Certainly, in Greene County, the soldier vote would have made no difference to the election's outcome. J. J. Purman reported that in Company A, 140th Pennsylvania Volunteers, the Greene County men held an election on October 14th, and "it was ascertained that the company stood about two-thirds Democratic to one-third Republican," a ratio that reflected county voters back home. Purman told the editors of the *Messenger* that the voting-age men of Company A cast forty-one votes for Lazear and twenty for Wallace. When the votes were counted for the whole company, including those not old enough to lawfully vote, the election results were sixty-eight Democrats versus thirty-four Republicans.[54] The *Waynesburg Messenger* called Wallace's charges "a sheer fabrication." For the Greene County Democratic newspaper, these "charges" were "too grave to be made lightly, and recklessly of their truth, as they doubtless are in this instance." "They may afford a grain of comfort to disappointed and sore-headed Abolitionists," the editors chided, "but it is at the sacrifice of honor and magnanimity on the part of our opponents."[55] What negotiations were concluded to calm the protest are unclear. Governor Andrew Curtin, however, certified Jesse Lazear's election in a proclamation signed on December 11, 1862.[56]

In October 1862, Dr. Alexander Patton, Democrat from Clarksville in Morgan Township, was elected Greene County's representative in the Pennsylvania Assembly. Dr. Patton was known for his unquestioned and unquestionable patriotism. A strong party man, it was believed that his intelligence, ability, and integrity made him a strong candidate. "No man in the country," reported the *Waynesburg Messenger,* "is more outspoken, and decided in opinion or purpose, or more incorruptibly honest."[57] At a Democrat County meeting in March that year, Dr. Patton made a resolution praising the then current assemblyman, Patrick Donley, whose term in office was expiring. Donley had been a solid representative for the county. As the 1862 legislative session closed, Donley could look back at having proposed and seen passed a law compensating the Greene County sheriff three dollars per day and three cents per mile for the transportation of prisoners sentenced by the county courts to state penitentiaries. In addition, he shepherded a law changing the township elections in the county from the third to the second Friday of each March.[58] Dr. Patton's resolution declared Donley "capable and efficient," having used "watchful care of the interests of his constituents and of the Commonwealth."[59] The election of Dr. Patton as Donley's replacement was viewed by the Democrats as extremely important. Pennsylvania's United States Senator David Wilmot's term was expiring on March 4, 1863. Wilmot, a radical Republican, was famous for the "Wilmot Proviso" that he introduced as a Congressman in 1848 which, if it had been adopted, would have prohibited the introduction of slavery into any territories gained from Mexico after the Mexican War. Since Wilmot's successor would be elected by the state legislature, the presence of Dr. Patton would help insure the election of a Democrat as the new Senator. This was accomplished when Charles R. Buckalew became the junior senator from Pennsylvania in January 1863. The senior Senator, Edgar Cowan from Westmoreland County, was a Republican.[60]

Buckalew's election, however, proved to be very close. The Republican caucus nominated Simon Cameron for the United States Senate seat. Stories were rampant about Cameron's efforts to persuade or bribe a Democratic legislator to abandon Buckalew and throw his vote over to the Republican minority in the Pennsylvania Assembly. Democrat Assemblyman, T. Jefferson Boyer, from Clearfield County, charged that Cameron had offered him twenty thousand dollars for his support. After the election was over, Dr. Patton noted that Buckalew had been chosen by a strict party vote. In the final tally, the Democratic candidate for Wilmot's vacant seat was elected by only a one vote majority.[61]

Shortly after taking his seat in the new Pennsylvania legislature in January 1863, Dr. Patton introduced a resolution on February 5, 1863, stating the Federal government had no right to request that Pennsylvania provide men or material for its war effort until Lincoln rescinded the Emancipation Proclamation. Dr. Patton noted that "the present bloody and devastating civil war could, and should have been averted, by the adoption of the Crittenden compromise, or by some other measure alike just and honorable to all sections of the country." Placing "the whole responsibility" for the war upon the "dominant party in Congress," Dr. Patton, speaking for many Peace Democrats throughout the state, declared that the President's act in freeing the slaves in the South was unconstitutional and unnecessarily changed the objective of the war from its original aim of preserving the Union.[62] The Republican *Huntingdon Globe* paraphrased Patton's resolution as "declaring that if the Administration persisted in weakening the rebels by taking from them the labor of the slaves, it can have no further claims upon the loyal State of Pennsylvania for men or other means of carrying on the war." The editor characterized Dr. Patton as providing aid and comfort for the rebels and advised that the Greene County representative "should be passed over the line" to the South.[63] The resolution did not pass, but George Turner at Bloomsburg University believes that Dr. Patton's action can be seen as a symptom of fear that the North would be inundated by freed Blacks from the South or that Lincoln and the Republicans were trying to impose racial equality between Blacks and Whites.[64]

Support for his thesis can be found in a series of resolutions adopted by a Democratic Party meeting in Davistown in Dunkard Township held on Saturday, March 8, 1863. John Stephenson, who served as president, with Jacob Shriver and J. Bussey as vice-presidents, and E. Chalfant serving as secretary, chaired the meeting. The committee on resolutions consisted of Samuel Hayes, A. Jamison, and William Knotts. The resolutions proposed by them and passed by the delegates at the meeting included support for the efforts being made by Jesse Lazear in Congress, but added that the Democrats of Dunkard Township were "opposed to any and all of the unconstitutional schemes of Abolitionism to equalize the negro and white races, either by sword or by proclamation."

Further, they resolved "that this government was made by white men and for white men, and that the negro has no part therein, as a citizen." Calling for support of the "Constitution as our fathers made it, and for the Union as it was, " the committee demanded that 'this bloody war'" be terminated "by fair, just and Constitutional compromises."[65]

At a Democratic Party meeting in Mapletown, in October 1862, moreover, the Dunkard Township delegates "decorated themselves with paw paw bushes, in imitation of the Southern Palmetto." While the Dunkard Township men marched in procession to the meeting, they "cheered loudly for Jeff. Davis, and threatened violence to anyone who should utter a syllable in favor of the Government, and actually halted to chastise a woman who had the courage and patriotism to express her preference for Abraham Lincoln." It was noted that the meeting was "quite large, and, in a certain sense, enthusiastic." Judge Samuel Gilmore of Uniontown, David Crawford, Esquire, and others, addressed the crowd by reciting "the anti-nigger and antiwar homilies, cooked up to suit the people."[66]

More evidence for Dr. Turner's thesis is a movement started by Greene County's Democratic newspaper for a petition banning free Blacks from immigrating to Pennsylvania in January 1863. The paper encouraged its readers to circulate and sign the proposed petition and forward it to Dr. Patton in Harrisburg. The petition printed in the paper deplored "the large influx of colored people from the South," and it stated that their "habits of indolence unsuit them for residence in an industrious and moral community." There was a fear, moreover, that "this class has largely increased not only the paupers in Poor Houses, but the criminal business of our Courts."[67] From Harrisburg, Dr. Alexander Patton reported from the Pennsylvania Assembly that such a bill would soon be passed:

> We will pass a bill in a few days, relative to the emigration of "American citizens of African descent" into our own State, but I presume it will fail in the Senate. There being a majority of negro worshippers in that body with that pink of political perfection and paragon of Abolition excellencies, George V. Lawrence at their head, what else can we look for? The action of the whole Republican party is directed to the benefit of the negro more than to that of their white brethren, and, of course, the whites must not look for beneficial legislation whilst they are in the ascendency in any of the departments of our State government.[68]

The Waynesburg Messenger, a Democratic newspaper, summed up the view of many Greene County Democrats in an article published on July 16, 1862. Purporting to be a conversation heard in the street by the reporter, the unidentified parties spoke as follows:

> "DEMOCRAT -- I am in favor of prosecuting the war to the utter putting down of the rebellion, and shall

sustain the Administration in all its efforts to enforce the laws, restore the Union as it was, and preserve the Constitution as it is. But I am opposed to frequent violations of the Constitution, and to unconditional and universal emancipation.

REPUBLICAN -- D__n the Constitution! -- What has it to do with the war? The 'war power' gives the President the right to arrest whoever he pleases and to suspend the writ of Habeas Corpus when he pleases, and gives Congress the right to emancipate the slaves, and I'm in favor of doing it if necessary."[69]

---

[1] Smith, p. 15.

[2] Powell, p. 172.

[3] *Daily Morning Post* (Pittsburgh), 18 May 1847, p. 2.

[4] *Lancaster Intelligencer*, 31 October 1848, p. 2.

[5] *Daily Morning Post* (Pittsburgh), 18 September 1852, p. 2.

[6] *Ibid,* 9 October 1854, p. 2.

[7] *Huntingdon Globe*, 13 June 1855, p. 3.

[8] *Pittsburgh Daily Gazette and Advertiser*, 23 July 1855, p. 2; *Daily Morning Post* (Pittsburgh), 23 July 1855, p. 2.

[9] *Huntingdon Globe*, 8 July 1857, p. 2.

[10] Philadelphia *Press*, 7 April 1865, p. 2; *Lancaster Intelligencer*, 21 May 1850, p. 2, 1 November 1853, p. 2; *Pittsburgh Daily Gazette and Advertiser*, 10 March 1855, p. 2, 4 March 1858, p. 2; *Waynesburg Messenger*, 17 February 1864, p. 3.

[11] Information on John Wells can be found in Samuel P. Bates, *History of Greene County, Pennsylvania*, p. 343; Hanna, p. 313; L.K. Evans, *Pioneer History of Greene County*, p. 166; and Smith, p. 173. John Wells' daughter, Ellen, married Congressman J. B. Donley in 1871. See Bates, p. 659.

[12] *Waynesburg Messenger*, undated clipping attached to letter from W. H.

Wells to Abraham Lincoln, 3 January 1859 (Abraham Lincoln Papers at the Library of Congress, Transcribed and Annotated by the Lincoln Studies Center, Knox College, Galesburg, Ill.), Series I, General Correspondence, 1833-1916.

[13] Wells to Lincoln, 3 January 1859.

[14] *Collected Works of Abraham Lincoln*, A. Lincoln to W. H. Wells, 8 January 1859, Vol. III, p. 349.

[15] *Waynesburg Messenger*, 28 August 1861, p. 3.

[16] *Ibid*, 5 March 1862, p. 3; 18 December 1861, p. 3.

[17] *Waynesburg Messenger*, 2 April 1862, p. 3.

[18] *Ibid*, 18 June 1862, p. 3.

[19] *Ibid*, 6 August 1862, p. 3.

[20] *Ibid*, 2 September 1863, p. 3.

[21] *Ibid*, 4 May 1864, p. 2.

[22] *Ibid*, 8 February 1865, p. 3.

[23] Bates, p. 659.

[24]Powell, pp. 173, 176.

[25] "Diary of Honorable James Lindsey," entry for 16 February 1861 (transcript of diary in collection of Cornerstone Genealogical Society, Waynesburg, Pennsylvania).

[26] *Daily Morning Post* (Pittsburgh), 27 October 1852, p. 3; *Lancaster Intelligencer*, 23 December 1856, p. 2; D. Kent Fonner, "'We Had Quite an Exciting Time . . . :' James Lindsey at the 1857 State Democratic Convention,'" *Cornerstone Clues*, Vol. 24, No. 3 (August 1999), pp. 75-78.

[27] Diary of James Lindsey, 2 January 1861.

[28] *Ibid*, 4 January 1861.

[29] *Ibid*, 5 January 1861.

[30] *Ibid*, 4 February 1861.

[31] *Ibid,* 5 March 1861.

[32] *Waynesburg Messenger*, 16 October 1861, p. 3.

[33] *Ibid,* 26 September 1861, p. 3.

[34] *Ibid,* 2 October 1861, p. 3.

[35] *Ibid,* 20 August 1862, p. 3.

[36] See Turner, pp. 409-423. Also see Harold M. Hyman, *A More Perfect Union: The Impact of the Civil War and Reconstruction on the Constitution* (Boston: Houghton Mifflin Company, 1975); Mark E. Neely, Jr., "The Civil War and the Two Party System," James M. McPherson, Ed., *"We Cannot Escape History:" Lincoln and the Last Best Hope of Earth* (Chicago: University of Illinois Press, 1995); Mark E. Neely, Jr., *The Fate of Liberty: Abraham Lincoln and Civil Liberties* (New York: Oxford University Press, 1991); Mark E. Neely, Jr., *The Union Divided: Party Conflict in the Civil War North* (Cambridge, MA: Harvard University Press, 2002); Grace Palladino, *Another Civil War: Labor, Capital, and the State in the Anthracite Regions of Pennsylvania, 1840-1868* (New York: Fordham University Press, 2006); J. G. Randall, *Constitutional Problems under Lincoln* (New York: D. Appleton & Company, 1926); Robert M. Sandow, *Deserter Country: Civil War Opposition in the Pennsylvania Appalachians* (New York: Fordham University Press, 2009); Jennifer L. Weber, *Copperheads: the Rise and Fall of Lincoln's Opponents in the North* (New York: Oxford University Press, 2006).

[37] "Jesse Lazear," *Biographical Directory of the United States Congress, 1774-Present* (http://bioguide.congress.gov/scripts/biodisplay.pl?index=L000154), retrieved 10 July 2011. Also see Hanna, pp. 104-106,276-277; Bates, pp. 459-460.

[38] *Daily Morning Post* (Pittsburgh, PA), 25 June 1858, p. 2.

[39] *Ibid.*

[40] *Ibid.*

[41] *Waynesburg Messenger*, 4 September 1861, p. 3.

[42] *Ibid.*

[43] *Waynesburg Messenger*, 23 July 1862, p. 3; 30 April 1862, p. 3; 1 October 1862, p. 3; 22 October 1862, p. 3.

[44] *Official Records of the War of the Rebellion* (O.R.), Series II, Vol. 1 (Washington, DC: Government Printing Office, 1889), p. 759.

[45] O.R., Series II, Vol. 1, p. 664.

[46] "Speech of Honorable Jesse Lazear," *The Congressional Globe*, 37th Congress, 3rd Session, Vol. 33, pt. 2 (Appendix), 28 February 1863, pp. 159-161.

[47] *Congressional Globe*, Vol. 34, pt. 3, 38th Congress, 1st Session, 31 May 1864, p. 2586.

[48] *Pennsylvania Daily Telegraph* (Harrisburg, PA), 1 December 1864, p. 2.

[49] Ibid, 13 October 1864, p. 2.

[50] *The Press* (Philadelphia), 4 October 1862, p. 1.

[51] *Waynesburg Messenger*, 8 October 1862, p. 3.

[52] *Pennsylvania Daily Telegraph* (Harrisburg, PA), 25 November 1862, p. 2.

[53] *Lancaster Intelligencer*, 4 November 1862, p. 2.

[54] *Waynesburg Messenger,* 5 November 1862, p. 2.

[55] *Waynesburg Messenger*, 5 November 1862, p. 3.

[56] *Pennsylvania Daily Telegraph*, 13 December 1862, p. 2.

[57] *Waynesburg Messenger,* 18 June 1862, p. 3.

[58] *Ibid,* 16 April 1862, p. 3.

[59] *Ibid,* 26 March 1862, p. 3.

[60] *Ibid,* 1 October 1862, p. 3.

[61] *Ibid,* 21 January 1863, p. 2; 28 January 1863, p. 3.

[62] *Journal of the House of Representatives of the Commonwealth of Pennsylvania, of the Session Begun at Harrisburg, on the Sixth Day of January, 1863* (Harrisburg: Singerly & Myers, State Printers, 1863), p. 167.

[63] *Huntingdon Globe,* 11 February 1863, p. 2.

[64] Turner, p. 414.

[65] *Waynesburg Messenger*, 11 March 1863, p. 2.

[66] *Pennsylvania Daily Telegraph* (Harrisburg, PA), 31 October 1862, p. 1.

[67] *Waynesburg Messenger,* 14 January 1863, p. 3.

[68] *Ibid,* 1 April 1863, p. 2.

[69] *Waynesburg Messenger*, 16 July 1862, p. 3.

Chapter IV: "All Quiet on the Border;" the Jones-Imboden Raid into West Virginia

The late spring and summer of 1863 was destined to be a trying time in Greene County, as it was for Pennsylvania and the rest of the country. It started on April 20 and April 21, 1863, when two columns of approximately 7000 Confederate troops made their way out of the Shenandoah Valley headed on a raid against the B&O Railroad facilities in western Virginia. A force of infantry, cavalry, and artillery, led by Brigadier General John D. Imboden headed toward the towns of Beverly, Philippi, and Grafton. Brigadier General William E. (Grumble) Jones led the second column composed of 3000 men, mostly cavalry. Jones was leading his detachment toward the railroad bridges on the Cheat River and the Monongehela River near Morgantown in Monongalia County. Arriving at Rowlesburg on the Cheat River on April 26, Jones was met by Major J. H. Showalter with two hundred fifty men from the 6th (West) Virginia Infantry. Showalter put up a strong defense, and Jones eventually skirted the Union position and moved on to Morgantown with 1500 men. In the meantime, Showalter, fearing for the safety of his small force, hastily retreated to Uniontown, Pennsylvania, taking with him five hundred men and four pieces of artillery. He proceeded from there to Connellsville, where he placed his troops on a train bound for Pittsburgh, intending to board a riverboat for Wheeling. Jones' force of 1500 Confederate cavalry occupied Morgantown at about two o'clock in the afternoon of April 27, 1863. Panic spread throughout western Pennsylvania and Wheeling.[1]

After occupying Morgantown, the rebels began searching the vicinity and making prisoners of certain citizens who were known to be strong Union supporters. The country home of the local provost marshal, Captain William Leazure, was burned, and at least three men were executed after firing in ambush on some of Jones' cavalry.[2] The three were identified as Lloyd Bell, "a prominent citizen and most devout Unionist," J.J. Jenkins, and Andrew Johnson. The raiders also captured Lieutenant Henry Bell and a man named Morrison. It was believed they were also to be shot for "bushwhacking" the Rebel column.[3]   One of the pro-Union men sought by the raiders, identified by the Wheeling *Daily Intelligencer* as a Colonel Boyers, a deputy marshal, rode north toward Waynesburg just as the Confederate cavalry approached his home. He lived two miles down the Monongahela River from Morgantown and rode all the way through Waynesburg, arriving in Washington, Pennsylvania about 11 o'clock that night. Morgantown resident and former United States senator from Virginia, W. T. Willey, escaped to Carmichaels. He was accompanied by another man identified as Squire Price. Willey sent a message to Waynesburg indicating that the rebel force was two thousand to four thousand men.   An emergency meeting was held at the Greene County Courthouse on Tuesday morning, April 28, 1863, at 2 o'clock A. M., to discuss what measures to take in regard to the danger posed by the Confederates in Morgantown. On a motion by "Colonel" R. W. Jones, a Committee of Safety was appointed. The committee was composed of John C. Flenniken, W. T. E. Webb, Alfred Myers, J. A. J. Buchanan, David Crawford, Joseph Wiley, and William A. Porter.   The committee was charged with commanding scouting parties, sounding the alarm bell, determining what action to take in the emergency, and to appoint a captain and two lieutenants to take charge of the town's arms and ammunition and to command any defense force raised.[4]   In the meantime, another rider left Waynesburg around the time of the meeting, bringing to Washington the news that Confederate cavalry was reported to be at Newtown [Kirby], only nine miles from Waynesburg.[5]

In Greensboro, Pennsylvania, a messenger from Morgantown exaggerated the Confederate army's strength as twenty thousand men, extending in a line of march twenty miles from Morgantown to Fairmount. *The Press* of Philadelpia noted, "The citizens of Greene and Fayette counties, in Pennsylvania, are disconcerted, and some of them on the borders are taking flight. Several have suffered loss by rebel scouts."[6]   At the Farmers and Drovers Bank, in Waynesburg, Cashier and Congressman Jesse Lazear began destroying $60,000 in F&D issued bank notes so they would not fall into Confederate hands.[7]   Republican newspapers reported that the leading citizens of the town decided that they would not try to defend Waynesburg. Congressman Lazear rode out eight miles with a flag of truce seeking the Rebel invaders and someone to whom he could surrender the town. He found no one after a diligent search.[8] Late in the evening of April 27, several trains that had been waiting at Cameron arrived in Wheeling with news that a bridge had been burned at Burton and rebel cavalry were seen twenty miles east of Cameron. The commander of the Union forces at Wheeling, Captain W. C. Thorpe of the 13th United States Infantry, became even more alarmed when it was mistakenly reported that Confederate cavalry was at Waynesburg.[9]

Judge James Lindsey, Rufus K. Campbell, and Samuel A. Porter made a reconnaissance down the road from Waynesburg to Morgantown on April 28, 1863. They reported finding twelve hundred to sixteen hundred rebels camped at Keck's farm, two miles from Morgantown. The three men encountered a squad of Confederate cavalry near Morgantown and were chased "a considerable distance and fired at." They all escaped unharmed.[10] "Colonel" R. W. Jones, senior editor of the *Waynesburg Messenger,* led a detachment "of some thirty-five or forty gallant spirits from Waynesburg" on a "glorious hunt and repulse" of a rebel force threatening to enter Greene County near Brown's Mills on the West Virginia side of Dunkard Creek, not far from Blacksville.[11]

On April 28, 1863, however, "Grumble" Jones, after destroying the turnpike suspension bridge over the Cheat River, had moved off to attack the garrison at Fairmont and search for Imboden near Clarksburg. Besides burning Captain Lazear's house, the raiders carried off two hundred horses from Morgantown and pillaged boots, drugs, hats, groceries, and various other goods from stores in the town. In Bridgeport, Henry Solomon White, and a detachment of Company N, Sixth (West) Virginia Infantry, received orders from the regiment's commander, Colonel N. Wilkinson, "to burn the railroad bridge and fall back on Fairmont to meet the rebels that were coming in by way of Morgantown." White stated that the men carried out the order and "rather reluctantly" made their first retreat. He noted that the civilians in the area were in a complete panic, and one Company N man, Linsy Moore, suffering with a fever, had to be left "behind at the mercy of the Confederate soldiers if they come in, which they surely will do."[12]

The ten-man detachment of Company N arrived at Fairmont at noon, April 28, 1863. The town was nearly deserted, and those few residents remaining were "frightened, thinking that raiders would be in soon." To defend the town and the 615-foot B&O Railroad suspension bridge over the Monongahela River at this point, White counted two companies of the 106th New York Infantry, twenty-five men from Company A, Sixth (West) Virginia Infantry, one company of Home Guards, and the ten men from Company N. The commanding officer in Fairmont, Captain Chamberlaine of the 106th New York, therefore, had two hundred thirty-four men to meet the approaching raiders led by Jones. All afternoon, the small defending force was haunted by various rumors of the location of Jones' Confederates. They spent part of the day drawn up in line of battle "thinking" the rebels "were up on us at every hour." That night, they were ordered to sleep on their arms and be prepared for any emergency before morning.[13]

At dawn on April 29, 1863, Jones' column had reached Fairmont. The Union defenders formed a battle line on the hill above the bridge. Jones split his command into three columns and soon had the small force at the bridge surrounded. White wrote that he and his comrades fought the Confederates "manfully" for nearly three hours, but "surrendered just in time to save ourselves from a grand charge which they were making." White, and two other defenders, had taken a position in a ravine near the river. One of the men with White, Fontaine Smith, was a resident of Fairmont and a strong Union man, "greatly outraged," who had equipped himself with a muzzle-loading squirrel rifle. The other man, John S. Barnes, served with White in Company N. During the course of the skirmish, Barnes was hit in the forehead, with the bullet passing along the top of his skull and out through the base of the rear of his neck. He recovered from the injury. White was in the process of taking a shot when he was hit in the right elbow, the bullet passing through the bones above and below the joint. After he was captured, White was taken to a basement of a building on the east side of Main and Quincy streets, where his wound was dressed by a local doctor, Dr. Eyster. After being paroled as a prisoner of war, White was left by his captors in the care of Mrs. W. D. Wilson in Fairmont. He later wrote that he would "never . . . forget her for her kindness." White listed the casualties in the affray as two Union men killed and six wounded. He was certain that Jones' men had suffered not less than sixteen killed and twenty wounded. After destroying the bridge over the Monongahela, and looting the town and taking every horse in the area "to the disgust of even their sympathizers," Jones led his column off toward Bridgeport "about midnight to the entire satisfaction of all parties."[14]

By May 6, 1863, *The Waynesburg Messenger* reported that the excitement "has almost entirely subsided."[15] The newspaper noted that Waynesburg's Committee of Public Safety had gotten the "home forces" in readiness, and Washington County had sent a company of infantry commanded by Captain Alexander Wishart. By Saturday, May 2, 1863, the alarm was over and the Washington County men went home. Under the headline, "All Quiet on the Border," the newspaper reported that the "imminent danger of a Rebel incursion" had passed. "At present," the *Messenger* assured its readers, "all is quiet, and all alarm allayed."[16]

As the spring turned to summer that year, however, with Lee's threatened invasion of Pennsylvania in June, Greene County again felt its vulnerability on the Mason-Dixon Line. On June 15, 1863, Judge Lindsey received a letter from Major General William T. H. Brooks, commander of the Department of the Monongahela in Pittsburgh, advising Lindsey to see that the people of Greene County were organized for defense and that representatives be sent to Pittsburgh to confer with Brooks regarding the threat to western Pennsylvania posed by Lee's army.[17] James Jennings at the *Messenger* received a letter from Pittsburgh advising him of the "excited and alarmed state of feeling" in the city. Thousands of workers were digging entrenchments for the defense of Pittsburgh, viewed as a likely target of the Confederates because of the arsenal and cannon foundry located there. The unnamed correspondent added:

> I do not know what may be done at home— whether anything or not: but I advise *you to get up a Company at once,* and to say to the people through the

paper, that they should organize Companies at once in all the townships. Arms and ammunition will be furnished them without delay. There is no doubt of this.[18]

On June 16, 1863, a company of Greene County volunteers was organized in Waynesburg, with L. R. McFann as Captain, George Inghram, First Lieutenant, Robert Adams, Jr., Second Lieutenant, and B. M. Blatchley as orderly sergeant. The men enlisted for the duration of "the emergency," and immediately made their way down the Monongahela River to Pittsburgh. Less than a week later General Brooks sent them back to Greene County after deciding there was no imminent danger posed to Pittsburgh. Still, he thanked the men for their prompt response, the company having been organized in only a few hours after the call for help. He also advised them to maintain their organization in case they were needed to protect the border. The *Brownsville Times* pointed to this company of volunteers from Greene County as proof of the falsity of charges of disloyalty "often made against the Democracy of noble little Greene." Of the one hundred men in the company, "all but about a dozen are Copperheads, as their opponents delight to call Democrats."[19]

In Clarksville, as soon as news of the Battle of Gettysburg reached the county, Dr. Alexander Patton, home from the state legislature, closed his medical practice and immediately made his way to the scene of the tragedy. For weeks, he stayed there, "ministering, without fee or reward, to the sick, the wounded and the dying, until he has been well-nigh exhausted." Certain the doctor would be elected for another term to the Pennsylvania assembly, the *Waynesburg Messenger* speculated that a "braver, and better, and more loyal heart than the Doctor's never beat under a big 'waistcoat.'"[20]

Yet, the newspapers reported something unsettling about the Morgantown raid that spring. *The Press*, at the time of the incident, stated, "The invaders seem to have been thoroughly posted by their sympathizers in Western Virginia, and some even in Western Pennsylvania. It has been asserted that a Pennsylvania lawyer escorted the rebels into Morgantown, and still acts as their guide, and the assertion is not deemed unreliable."[21] *The Reporter and Tribune* from Washington,

71

Pennsylvania, however, shed more light on the subject in a piece, published on May 13, 1863, under the headline: "A Genuine Copperhead." It seemed that the Uniontown papers were reporting that Major Showalter, who had again occupied Morgantown, captured and brought with him to Uniontown a man named David Lilly. Lilly was accused of being a spy for the Confederate raiders and a traitor who led the rebels around Morgantown to the homes of prominent Union men. Moreover, Lilly had been seen in Uniontown a few days before the raid, leading to speculation that he was scouting for a foray into Fayette County. The paper described Lilly as "a Democrat of the Vallandigham stripe," referring to a notorious Peace Democrat from Ohio who was eventually banished to the South. The most curious thing about Lilly, however, was that he was a resident of Pennsylvania and a member of the Waynesburg bar.[22]

---

[1] Edward G. Longacre, *Mounted Raids of the Civil War* (New York: A.S. Barnes and Company, 1975), pp. 123-147; Robert B. Boehm, "The Jones-Imboden Raid through West Virginia," *Civil War Times Illustrated*, Vol. 3, No. 2 (May 1964), pp. 14-21; OR, Series I, Vol. 25, pt. 1, pp. 90-137.

[2] *The Press* (Philadelphia), 4 May 1863, p. 2; O.R., Series I, Vol. 25, pt. 1, p. 126.

[3] *Evening Telegraph* (Harrisburg), 4 May 1863, p. 1.

[4] *Waynesburg Messenger,* 29 April 1862, p. 3.

[5] *Daily Intelligencer* (Wheeling), 29 April 1863, p.2; *The Reporter and Tribune* (Washington, PA), 29 April 1863, p. 2.

[6] *The Press* (Philadelphia), 4 May 1863, p. 2.

[7] *Evening Telegraph* (Harrisburg), 4 May 1863, p. 1.

[8] *Weekly Mariettian* (Marietta, PA), 6 June 1863, p. 2.

[9] *Daily Intelligencer* (Wheeling), 29 April 1863, p. 2; O.R., Series I, Vol. 25, pt. 2, p. 281; also see dispatch from Campbell Tarr, state treasurer of WV and Marshal E. M. Norton in *The Pittsburgh Post*, 29 April 1863, p. 3.

[10] *Waynesburg Messenger,* 29 April 1863, p. 3.

[11] *Ibid,* 13 January 1864, p. 3.

[12] Diary of Henry Solomon White, 26 April 1863.

[13] *Ibid*, 28 April 1863.

[14] *Ibid*, 29 April 1863 and "Memo" attached thereto

[15] *Waynesburg Messenger*, 6 May 1863, p. 3.

[16] *Ibid.*

[17] *Ibid*, 17 June 1863, p. 3.

[18] *Ibid.*

[19] *Brownsville Times* as quoted by the *Waynesburg Messenger*, 1 July 1863, p. 3.

[20] *Waynesburg Messenger*, 22 July 1863, p. 3.

[21] *The Press* (Philadelphia), 4 May 1863, p. 2.

[22] *The Reporter and Tribune* (Washington, PA), 13 May 1863, p. 2.

Home Front Vignette: "The People's Park"

[During the Civil War, civic pride in Greene County continued to provide improvements in the community as demonstrated by an article published in the Waynesburg Messenger on March 18, 1863 calling for creation of a park on the commons on the North Side of Waynesburg.]

"We like the suggestion in the subjoined article, sent us by a lady friend. If our good people will all join in the undertaking she proposes, we can have a Park here which will be a lasting memorial to the taste and enterprise of our citizens:

The People's Park

Friends and neighbors, do you wish to have among us that which will add beauty and attraction to our town, comfort and pleasure to her children – a place of resort for pleasure parties and picnics, and cooling shade for our little ones, when weary of their plays and studies, to rest beneath? If so, come one, come all, and lend a hand in planning a beautiful park, which will yield us all this and more, and add to the worth of property, throughout our town. You are invited to come the 27th of March, or if not convenient, 28th, and bring as many trees as you please, with stakes and boards to box. Come with your teams, all that can, and assist in laying out a circular carriage road around our Common, which, I am sure, will be of special interest to young gentleman, as a ride, drive or walk, shaded by beautiful trees, and preferable to one on the barren commons. Gentlemen from the country are invited to come. You will probably send children here to school who, as they enjoy the shade and look upon the beauty of a Park, will bless you for your labor. May we not look to the Council of our borough to contribute something towards the building of one or two small bridges, for the accommodation of the people living on the

North side of the common? Certainly there should be public spirit enough in our good Council for this. The ladies are ready to prepare a nice supper and entertain you with music, at the College, after your work is done. Dinners will be provided at our homes for those that come in the morning, and will stay. May we, on the 27th, see a spirit of enterprise, taste and good feeling manifested throughout our community.
PRO BONO PUBLICO."

Chapter V: ". . . To Know What It is To Be a Soldier . . ."

It has been estimated that 1800 men from Greene County served in at least forty different military units of the Union army, including several hundred who served in Northern regiments raised in western Virginia.[1] Greene County volunteers composed Company F, First Pennsylvania Cavalry; Company I, Eighth Pennsylvania Reserve Infantry; Company K, Fifteenth Pennsylvania Cavalry; Companies A, C, and G, Eighteenth Pennsylvania Cavalry; Company F, Eighty-Fifth Pennsylvania Infantry; Company A, One Hundred Fortieth Pennsylvania Infantry; Company A, One Hundred Sixty-Eighth Pennsylvania Infantry; and Company F, Seventh (West) Virginia Infantry. In addition, Greene County recruits were found scattered throughout various companies of the Eleventh Pennsylvania Infantry, the Fourteenth, Sixteenth, and Twenty-Third Pennsylvania Cavalry regiments, and the Sixty-First, One Hundred Sixteenth, and One Hundred Twenty-Third Pennsylvania Infantry regiments. Other men from the area enlisted in companies of the First (West) Virginia Cavalry, the First, Third, Fourth, Sixth, Eleventh, Twelfth, Thirteenth, Fourteenth, and Fifteenth (West) Virginia Infantry regiments. Greene County men even served in Company I, Second Colorado Cavalry, Company I, Seventy-Eighth Illinois Infantry, and in the United States Colored Troop service.[2]

Although not as numerous as volunteers from other counties of the state, Greene County men were generally complimented on their appearance as soldiers. The Pursley Guards, for example, were described as "No. 1 men—men who are influenced by pure, patriotic motives—and should they enter the service, will give a good account of themselves." Another company from Waynesburg recruited for the Eighty-fifth Pennsylvania was "composed of vigorous and gallant young fellows, and will do credit to the county."[3] Captain McCullough's "Greene County Rifles," upon arrival in Pittsburgh in September 1862, were described as "all able, strapping fellows, and many of them over six feet in height."[4]

The *Pittsburgh Gazette* believed that McCullough's recruits were "fine material for soldiers—young, lively, active and strong." "They have evidently been accustomed to hard work," the paper added, "and they all know how to handle a horse."[5] Another Pittsburgh newspaper agreed that Greene County boys were well suited to the cavalry. "A great number of volunteers" from Greene County were "in the cavalry service." "They are for the most part excellent horsemen," the article continued, "and in every engagement in which they have taken part have acquitted themselves in the handsomest manner."[6] Even the county's drafted men were reported to be "nearly all fine looking, muscular fellows," who "will make first-rate soldiers."[7]

For the most part, these Greene County soldiers were raw recruits when they entered the war. Although some had training as members of local county militia units, many went into the ranks with little to guide their expectations. William Silveus, for example, having enlisted in Company I, 8th Pennsylvania Reserve Infantry, on August 25, 1862, and being mustered into service at Harrisburg on September 8, 1862, less than two weeks later was camped with the regiment in Maryland on the Antietam Battlefield. Silveus described for his wife his initial introduction to soldiering after leaving Washington, D.C.:

> We left the city last Saturday and marched every day about 10 miles and camped out wherever we could catch it and whatever we wanted to eat we took. Last Sunday night one of our squad shot a pig and made a roast of it, although I didn't eat any of it. I won't eat anything that is stolen.[8]

As the recruits continued across the Maryland countryside, Silveus noted that they "crossed two battlefields and I tell you that it was a hard sight." About ten miles from the 8th Pennsylvania's camp, he described his first look at a battlefield hospital:

> We also stopped at a hospital and that was the hardest sight I ever saw. Some had their legs off and some their arms and some their hands, and one rebel had both legs

off above the knee. If you was here, you could see as high as 100 or 200 ambulances all in one train a hauling the wounded [to] the hospital.[9]

To his brother, Joe Silveus, he wrote, "I begin to know what it is to be a soldier, although I like it far better than I expected to."

After reaching the regiment, Silveus had some difficulty adjusting to the lack of regular communication from home. In an undated letter addressed to his wife, Mary, he chastised her for not writing to him:

> Once more I will write to you, but it is a going to be the last time until I get one from you. I do think a little hard of you that you don't write to me. I have not got one little sheet of you. Yet you don't know how I feel when the mail comes in and all the other boys get to hear from home and I have to stand back and look on. Now Mary do write if it ain't more than two lines. We have had some very hard marching of late. I stood it tolerable well. I am not so very well at this time but hope I may be well ere this reaches you and hope you may be well. Tell Mother and Joe that I want them to write.
>
> So no more at this time but my love to you.[10]

Captured at Fredericksburg, Virginia, on December 13, 1862, William Silveus contracted typhoid fever and died at Camp Parole, Maryland, on January 12, 1863. He is buried at the Annapolis National Cemetery in Maryland.

William Thomas Minor, son of L. L. Minor, was captured with Silveus at Fredericksburg. In a letter to his father, Minor described in great detail the experience of being captured and held at Libby Prison. As the assault of the Pennsylvania Reserves was pushed back he noticed that his brigade did not retreat in regular order but in pieces as sometimes a squad of ten or twelve men, then a company, or part of a regiment would fire and then break for the rear. At one point when he looked for Company I, he found that they had all gone. With bullets flying thick through the air he made a dash back thirty or forty yards to a ditch where he came upon Silveus. He said he told Silveus

78

they would be killed or captured, and no sooner made the statement then the Rebels appeared on the bank of the ditch and ordered them out. They were taken to the rear of the Confederate lines, where they had to make their way through a storm of canister and shell being fired by the Union artillery. They spent a couple nights just a few miles back of the lines, subsisting on a ration of a tin cup of flour per man until they were marched to the railroad and taken to Richmond. He noted they were treated well by the guards without any insults or harsh words to any man. When they arrived at the prison, it was a very cold and windy night. The column of prisoners was being processed two at a time, and some of the men had to stand in the street all night. Once inside, he noted that he was kept in a large room with about two hundred others. He slept on the floor and rations consisted of a tin of rice soup and half a loaf of bread in the morning and the same at night. They also received a small piece of fresh beef every other day. Minor remembered:

> I have gone through a great many hardships during the war, but nothing can compare with the three weeks I spent in prison. All sorts of characters, yelling, swearing and singing, from daylight until late in the night—with the floor alive with lice, and many of the men very sick—amongst them poor Sylveus.[11]

Silveus was confined in a different room. When Minor got to see him a few days later he was delirious but recognized Minor. The sick man lay on the bare floor without a blanket or any covering. His illness had settled in his lungs, causing a severe cough. Minor described the pitiful sight:

> It would have made you feel very sorry to have seen the poor man, trembling all over, his mind wandering, covered with vermin, talking to Mary, (his wife's name I believe,) the yelling and swearing like fiends, and smoking strong pipes under his very nose. Milton Johns, another member of our company, who was then taken prisoner, was in the same room, and did all he could for him.[12]

After the men were paroled, Minor saw Silveus one last time in the hospital on their boat. By that time, he noted that the man was "very low, and unable to talk so I could understand him."[13]

Silveus' brother-in-law, Albert Mildred, was the son of Charles Hart Mildred and Nancy Botkins Mildred. Mildred enlisted with the first rush of volunteers following President Lincoln's call after the fall of Fort Sumter in April 1861. The response in Pennsylvania had been so large that the federal government did not require the services of all the earliest volunteers. Accordingly, Governor Andrew Curtin called on the Pennsylvania legislature to permit the creation of a state "reserves corps" for defense of Pennsylvania's southern border. These men were formed into thirteen reserve regiments of infantry, one reserve regiment of cavalry, and a reserve regiment of light artillery. Officially designated as the "Reserve Volunteer Corps of the Commonwealth," the Pennsylvania Reserve Volunteer Corps, as it came to be known, was commanded by a West Point graduate and veteran of the Seminole and Mexican Wars, George Archibald McCall of Philadelphia, with the rank of major general of Pennsylvania Volunteers. Albert Mildred was mustered into Company I of the 8th Pennsylvania Reserves on June 20, 1861. He served throughout the war until the 8th Pennsylvania was mustered out on May 24, 1864.[14]

After initial drill and instruction at recruit camps near Pittsburgh, Mildred accompanied the newly-formed regiment when it was ordered to Washington, DC, on July 20, 1861, proceeding by rail from Pittsburgh to Washington by way of Harrisburg and Baltimore. At that time, the 8th Pennsylvania Reserves Regiment was commanded by Colonel George S. Hays, a former prothonotary of Allegheny County. Company I, recruited at Waynesburg, Greene County, Pennsylvania, was commanded by Captain Silas M. Baily, who was also mustered into service on June 20, 1861. Baily was subsequently promoted to the rank of Major on June 4, 1862. Wounded at the Battle of Gaines' Mill, June 27, 1862, Baily eventually was promoted to the rank of Colonel and handed command of the regiment on March 1, 1863. Colonel Hays resigned his commission after being severely injured at the Battle of Glendale (White Oak Swamp), on June 30, 1862, when his horse was torn to pieces by a cannon shot. By the end of the war, March 13, 1865, Baily received the rank of Brevet Brigadier General. When Baily was promoted to Major, command of Company I was handed to 1st Lieutenant John M. Kent, who was subsequently promoted to Captain on June 16, 1862. Wounded at the Battle of Fredericksburg in December 1862 and the Wilderness in May 1864, Captain Kent was mustered out with the regiment on May 24, 1864.

At least two of Private Mildred's letters written to his mother have survived. The first letter was written from Camp Tennally, located near Tennallytown, Maryland. An assembly area and training center for the Pennsylvania reserve regiments, the 8th Pennsylvania was ordered there on August 2, 1861. At that time, the regiment was assigned to the First Brigade of the Pennsylvania Reserve Division. The brigade was commanded by Brigadier General John F. Reynolds who later commanded the First Corps of the Army of the Potomac and was killed by a sniper on the first day of the Battle of Gettysburg. Mildred received his first taste of soldiering in the field when the 8th Pennsylvania was sent from camp for several days to reinforce the 7th Pennsylvania Reserves on picket duty at Great Falls, on the Potomac River. Mildred refers to this experience in his first letter, noting that "our officers place a good deal of confidence in me." When he returned to Camp Tennally, Mildred found the place buzzing with rumors of movements into Virginia. The 8th Pennsylvania, however, did not leave Camp Tennally until October 9, 1861, when they joined with the rest of the Pennsylvania reserve regiments in marching across the Chain Bridge from Washington, D.C., into northern Virginia. The command subsequently moved into winter quarters at Camp Pierpont near Langley, Virginia. It was from this camp that Mildred wrote the second letter in February, 1862:

"CampTenley [sic] Aug 28th 1861

Dear Mother
It is with great pleasure that I seat myself to answer your letter which came to hand in due time in which i was glad to hear from you that you was well and hope that this will still find you enjoying the same good blessings

I received your letter day before yesterday and would have answered it sooner but we had to go out on picket guard and did not get back last night at dusk the place where we was stationed was about 4 miles from our camp I put the night in scouting as there was a scouting party sent out and I was picked as one of the party we met with no adventures however as we could get no Prisoners Our officers place a good deal of Confidence in me as they generally pick on me to undertake anything that way we are expecting marching orders any minute as the order was last night to hold ourselves in readiness to march at a minutes warning So we have our provisions cooked and all ready to march where we will have to go I do not know but I think that we will have to cross the chain bridge over into Virginia as I expect we will have a small brush over there Harris Smith is still at the Hospital the boys say that he is well enough but I suppose that he will have no fighting to do while he is there I suppose that Nelson Thomas told plenty of lies by what Mrs. Watson wrote to Will but you need not believe a word he says as he was the worst man in our whole company and was dishonorably discharged on account of his bad conduct we have a nice place to incamp here we have everything that is good to eat Harpers company is here David Rhinehart was here last night as Asa Leonard is well he wants you when you write to let me know how Asa folks are getting along and then I want them to let me know how my folks are getting along so we can hear how you all are tell Jess Fordyce that I want him to write to me but I must bring my letter to a close tell all of them that I want them to write give my love to all and receive a share from your ever loving son

A. Mildred

Please write as soon as you receive this and give me all the news
Direct yours to A Mildred company I 8th Reg Pa Res Corps in care of Capt. SM Bailey"[15]

A few months later, Mildred wrote to his mother from Camp Pierpont near Langley, Virginia. His patriotism clearly shines through his writing:

"Nancy Mildred

Camp Pierpont Feb 18th 1862

Dear mother

Your letter came to hand last evening by which I was truly glad to hear from you that you was well this finds me in good health and I hope that it may find you enjoying the same good blessing. You said that you did not get any letters from me I do not know what is the reason as I am always being punctual in answering them I was sorry to hear of Libs ill health and of her grieving after Jo but I think when she gets the news we have here it will make her heart leape for joy Oh the soldiers are in such good spirits as we have such glorious news Within the last few weeks we have gained glorious victories. We have taken forts cities and some 25,000 prisoners besides some of their head generals. Even now their fate is sealed before two months the flag of the union will be waving over every rampart of the Southern Confederacy and then how happy will be our meeting husbands will be restored to their weeping wives sons to their fond parents and parents to their children and how happy will each one feel one to know that he has done his duty as a soldier to his country and the others proud to have such husbands and sons and brothers. Well mother I am glad to hear that you had got the money safe it will not be very long until we get paid again and then I will send you some more now I will try and give you some of the news about camp well we have been laying about camp all winter doing nothing except occasionally standing piquet which comes on our company about one every 15 days I was on camp guard night before last It is very bad underfoot now as there is a sleet underfoot which makes it very bad walking but while writing I hear the booming of cannon and the cheering of men I suppose we have heard more good news but I do not know what it is well mother I must bring my letter to a close as I believe I have given you all the news but I want you to answer this letter immediately and give my respects to all relations tell tell [sic] William to write also Martha tell Mary and Lib I would like to hear from them I want you to tell me what has become of Nancy as I have written her several letters and have never received any answer but I must close my respects to all friends no more but remain your affectionate son

Albert Mildred

PS write immediately and give me all the news. Farewell"[16]

In his second letter, Mildred is probably referring to news received in camp about General Grant's successful capture of Fort Henry on the Tennessee River on February 6, 1862, and Fort Donelson on the Cumberland River in Tennessee on February 16, 1862. The surrender of Nashville followed shortly on February 23, 1862. Another Greene County soldier, Henry Solomon White, with the Sixth (West) Virginia Infantry, also commented on the good news coming out of Tennessee that winter. In his diary on February 6, 1862, he wrote:

> The news reached us today of the capture of Fort Henry on the Cumberland River. I think we will have good news from that quarter every day until they capture Nashville. Anyhow, when they take that place, secession is gone up in Tennessee—may it come soon . . . .[17]

Although mistaken about the capture of Generals Johnson, Buckner, and Pillow, White, in Littleton, (West) Virginia, was excited about the fall of Fort Donelson:

> February 18th. Littleton. This morning our Company was wild with enthusiasm, having received the glorious

84

intelligence of the capture of Fort Donelson and 15,000 prisoners, including Generals Johnson, Buckner, and Pillow.[18]

The Sixth (West) Virginia Infantry was used primarily for provost duty and to guard various points on the B&O Railroad. Henry Solomon White, therefore, had a good opportunity to observe the routine of army life. He was an intelligent observer, and his diary contains a clear and well-written account of the experiences of the men of Company N who were his comrades. He noted, for example, that one day Captain John Kenney issued the men a part of their new equipment. "Today," he wrote, "we drew knapsacks, shirts, drawers, socks, blanket, pantaloons, canteens, gum shawls, shoes, and caps." As new recruits, some "of the boys were very well pleased with their new clothes. They thought they were tall soldiers."[19] Two days later, the men were issued their four-button fatigue coats, "blouses," and got their first taste of army rations:

> Our rations came and we must now go to our death on bread and flitch. The boys don't like the look of our fare but must take it root hog or die. I think they will get over their dainty tastes.[20]

On October 10, 1861, White joined thirty other men from Company N as volunteers to leave their camp at Burton by train to guard bridges at Littleton. He remarked that "some of the boys never had been on a train before. You may bet they were pleased with their ride." As the men began their guard duties on the railroad and scouting the surrounding area to "find where the secesh [sic] men stay," White stated that the "Company [is] in fine spirits."[21] At Littleton, the men were divided into "messes" and were boarded in private homes belonging to Freeman Hunt and Armstrong Hostuttler. When the men had been in the service two months, White found that "Most of us are well satisfied, some are getting a little sick of a soldier's life."[22] On the night of November 15, 1861, one of the men of Company N became notable for his marksmanship. Corporal Charles Woodruff had sent another corporal to relieve the guard. The man discharged his weapon at a person he saw lurking in the dark. When the results of his effort were examined, however, it was determined that he had fired at "nothing but a mile post," which he "badly wounded in the face."[23]

One problem faced by many soldiers in the war, including those recruited from Greene County, was the subject of pay. Henry Solomon White wrote that Company N did not sign their first pay muster until February 3, 1862, after serving over four months:

> Littleton. Today the Company were amused by having the privilege of signing the first pay roll since they entered the service. We have not seen one cent of Uncle Sam's money yet but hope to and that very soon. The men have all been out of heart in reference to their money and I think myself we have ben[sic] treated badly about our pay. Some of our men's families need their money very badly.[24]

By February 10, 1862, he noted that the men were "anxious" about "the appearance of a paymaster of this department."[25] On February 18, White remarked, "We expected our pay today but have not received it yet, but I suppose it will come tomorrow." By Washington's Birthday, White concluded, "There is something strange about our money or the reason the paymaster doesn't come around to pay us off." On March 8, the company was issued new fatigue coats, and White was certain that everything was "right now but our money and that appears to keep out of our sight." Another pay roll was signed March 12, but according to White, "the good Lord knows of what account it will be to us." The paymaster, "a very fine looking man" who White believed "will attend to his business better than that old crazy one," finally appeared in Littleton on March 15, 1862. White and his comrades received pay for five months and six days. The "boys are all in good spirits."[26]

For young men who had lived in isolated rural areas, army camp life brought the serious issue of disease, including some dangerous childhood infections. The subject of health played prominently in soldier correspondence and journals. In

November 1861, Henry Solomon White wrote that measles had struck the company. White himself was suffering with the disease, but his brother, William Thomas White, and a number of others were "very bad with them."[27] In February 1862, some of the men had developed mumps.[28] By summer, Captain Kenney escorted several men of Company N with camp illnesses to a hospital established in Grafton. On November 15, 1862, White remarked that the company had two men in the hospital and several in camp with jaundice. The captain was "very sick" with "rheumatism in the back."[29] When writing to his sister, S. Hill of Company F, 1st Pennsylvania Cavalry, was careful to inform her from his camp near Langley, Virginia, that he "never had better health than I have at the present." Moreover, "with few exceptions the health of our company has been extremely good."[30]

In addition to overcrowded and unsanitary conditions in camp, the severe physical strains of battlefield campaigning often contributed to a breakdown in a young soldier's health. D. S. Hopkins of Company A, 140th Pennsylvania Infantry, remembered leaving their winter quarters at Fort Welch, in front of Petersburg, Virginia, at four o'clock in the morning on December 9, 1864, in intensely cold weather, to march six or seven miles toward the left of the line until they met a Confederate force near Hatcher's Run. After "a severe little engagement for about 1 hour," the Rebels fell back, and Hopkins and his comrades held their position until the next afternoon. In the meantime, the Union soldiers were buried in six inches of snow brought on by a "severe snow storm and sleet." Hopkins wrote, "We suffered from the cold as we did not then have our tents to protect us from the cold storm." That day, as they returned to camp at Fort Welch, the snow-covered road turned to "mud and water half knee deep and we had a hard trip one that we had no desire to repeat." Back in camp, Hopkins was kept busy that winter "doing picket and guard duty working on fortifications policing and etc." By February 28, 1865, he had become ill and was sent to the Union hospital at City Point, Virginia, followed by a series of hospitals until he was discharged from the army from a hospital in Germantown, Pennsylvania, and started home on July 11, 1865.[31]

One of the most unfortunate causes of wounds and death

for soldiers in all eras were accidents. J. P. Crawford, from Carmichaels, was discharged from Company F, 1st Pennsylvania Cavalry, after he was severely kicked in the face by a vicious horse. The *Messenger* described Crawford as "an excellent young man" who "would no doubt have risen to prominence had he continued in the service."[32] Sergeant Major J. L. Ingrahm of Company I, 8th Pennsylvania Reserves Infantry, wrote a letter from Camp Pierpont, Virginia, on December 16, 1861, describing the accidental death of Richard Morris from Greene County. Company I had been sent out on picket duty a couple miles from camp. A few hours later, Captain Baily heard a rifle shot from the picket line and hurried to the post to determine the cause of the discharge. He was horrified to find Morris lying on the ground, shot in the head. Silas Chapman stood nearby with a look of despair at the result of the shot from his rifle. It was decided that the two men, close friends, had met each other on the picket line and began playing or maneuvering with their guns. Chapman's rifle accidently discharged, and Morris was hit. He died the next day, despite the best efforts of the regimental surgeon.[33]

A welcome break from army routine, depending on the circumstances, often occurred at holidays like Christmas. Henry Solomon White described the first Christmas he spent in the army while stationed at Littleton, Virginia:

> December 25, 1861. Christmas evening we began to prepare for Christmas spree at Armstrong Hostutler's. Fine a lot of turkeys were furnished by Lt. Parkerson and the messes furnished such rations as were necessary for the dinner. Misses Hostutler and Misses Owen being the cooks furnished such vegetables as were needed and at half past three the dinner was ready. About 40 ate dinner and then prepared for a dance. A row was raised in the evening which came very near spoiling the party. Finally all passed off and the gentlemen brought in the ladies for a dance – a fine looking lot of ladies were present. Dance kept up till late hour. A number of the Burton boys came down to participate in dance. Everything moved off with perfect tranquility this evening, it being the first Christmas evening spent in

camp by any of us.[34]

D. S. Hopkins remembered that on November 25, 1864, his company along with the whole Second Corps of the Army of the Potomac was given a Thanksgiving dinner by the citizens of New York. For Hopkins, the meal "was a grand treat."[35] War weariness can be read, however, in Henry Solomon White's description of Christmas in 1862:

> This is Christmas day. We are trying to enjoy ourselves as best we can. This is the second Christmas we have spent in camp. Our only hope is that by next year the war may be over and that those who are now absent from their homes and families may return to their family and homes of felicity and untold happiness.[36]

Wounded men often suffered terribly during the hours and days spent on a battlefield waiting for assistance. First Lieutenant J. Jackson Purman, Company A, 140th Pennsylvania Infantry, was shot in the left leg during the severe fighting in the Wheat Field at Gettysburg on July 2, 1863. Purman and Orderly Sergeant J. M. Pipes were in the process of retreating through the field when they were stopped by a wounded man from Company B crying for help. The two of them, with the Confederate battle line hot on them, picked up the man and moved him to the shelter of some rocks. At that point, Purman was hit in the leg. He described the wound as at first being "very like the shock of an electric battery." Shortly afterwards, though, "acute pain follows, and you know that a missile has passed through the tender flesh of your body." He found that the he had been hit about four inches above the ankle, the ounce lead ball crushing both bones in his lower leg. He lay in the tangled wheat surrounded by dead and wounded comrades and Confederates as the two sides continued to dispute possession of the field. During the night, he listened to the occasional cries and groans of the wounded. Lack of water soon brought on dehydration, and the morning only brought renewed firing from both sides. Eventually, his right leg was also hit by a bullet passing between his knee and ankle. In desperate need of water, he convinced a Confederate to bring a canteen to him and attempt to drag him out of the field and into the woods where the Rebel line was located. After the Union troops regained the position on the afternoon of July 3, Purman was taken to a field hospital where he received the attention of an army surgeon. An interesting side note to Purman's experience is the fact that he was placed in the care of the home in Gettysburg of Mary Withrow. Purman was ministered back to health by the woman's tender care, and later the couple were united in marriage.[37]

A look at the statistics on the number of deaths of Greene County Civil War soldiers is indeed "chilling."[38] Of the 1800 county men who served in the Northern army, 352 died from various causes, including 129 deaths from battlefield wounds, 163 deaths from disease or accidents, and 60 men who died in Rebel prison camps like Andersonville in Georgia and Libby Prison in Virginia.[39] It has been calculated that one of every nine Union soldiers in the United States died during the Civil War.[40] This is a mortality rate of about eleven per cent. For Greene County soldiers the ratio is nearly doubled to about twenty per cent or one death for every five men from Greene County who served in the war. To put this number in perspective, of the three "classmates" from Hopkin's Mill who enlisted in Company A, 140th Pennsylvania Infantry, in 1864, two, John Simpson and Job Smith, died on battlefields in Virginia before serving in the army even six months. Moreover, these figures do not include the number of men who died premature deaths after the war because of serious health problems brought on by complications from battlefield wounds or camp illnesses. The numbers also do not indicate the number of men returning to Greene County with missing limbs. J. J. Purman lost his left leg at Gettysburg. James M. Pipes lost an arm near Ream Station, Virginia. Isaac Scherich lost an arm at Opequan Creek, Virginia.

The first Greene County soldier killed in action during the Civil War was Jesse Taylor, a six foot, two inch, farmer from the Jollytown area. Taylor served in Company F, 7th (West) Virginia infantry. On October 26, 1861, the 7th (West) Virginia was included in a force of two thousand infantry and a company of cavalry, commanded by General Benjamin F. Kelley, advancing toward Romney, Virginia. After marching about thirteen miles, the detachment stopped to wait to be joined by the 4th Ohio Infantry. During the break, Joshua Rice, from Jollytown, took time to relax with two of his fellow mess mates in Company F, Jesse Taylor and Jefferson Dye. Taylor was in a playful mood, telling his friends he was going to catch the rebel cannonballs and throw them back. Later, after the column was joined by the Fourth Ohio, the three men were able to cook breakfast near Patterson Creek, where the force marching to Romney was increased by the arrival of the 8th Ohio Infantry and three pieces of artillery. As the Union force neared within two miles of Romney, the Confederates opened fire with a single artillery piece positioned in a cemetery overlooking the river. The gun was part of a rear guard covering the withdrawal of the main Confederate force in the town. As the Seventh continued to press forward toward the enemy position, a shell burst near Company F and Jesse Taylor was struck in the throat by a fragment. His comrades in Company F fashioned a coffin for the unfortunate man, and Jefferson Dye was permitted to accompany Taylor's remains by train to Burton, Virginia. Dye met Taylor's family at the Burton station and helped unload the rough-hewn box. When the women observed bloodstains on the side of the coffin, they burst into tears.[41]

As the war continued, the "boys" from Greene County serving in the armies of the Union were fast becoming "men." As they matured, they became military professionals who better understood the job they had been handed. They also came to better understand the stakes at risk in this war. G. William Pratt, whose family lived in Jefferson, Pennsylvania, was serving in Memphis, Tennessee, where a force of three divisions was being organized under the command of Major General William Sherman. Pratt expected that his regiment would soon be headed for Vicksburg by way of Jackson, Mississippi. Writing to his friend, A. L. Myers, Pratt expressed a sentiment that was no doubt shared by other Greene County soldiers:

> I tell you, Myers, that I am fast loosing[sic] what little mercy I once possessed for traitors & their sympathizers. When men Dare not insult us, there[sic] women & Children offer there[sic] insults. The men Dare not open

there[sic] mouths, if they did, we'd be unto them.[42]

[1] Smith, p. 27.

[2] Bates, *History of Greene County*, p. 457.

[3] *Waynesburg Messenger*, 9 October 1861, p. 3.

[4] *Pittsburgh Chronicle* as quoted by the *Waynesburg Messenger*, 10 September 1862, p. 3

[5] *Pittsburgh Gazette,* 21 October 1862, p. 3.

[6] *Pittsburgh Chronicle* as quoted by the *Waynesburg Messenger,* 29 October 1862, p. 3.

[7] *Waynesburg Messenger,* 29 October 1862, p. 3.

[8] William Silveus to Mary Silveus, 19 September 1862 (D. Kent Fonner collection); *Cornerstone Clues*, Vol. XX, #1 (February 1995), p. 17.

[9] *Ibid.*

[10] William Silveus to Mary Silveus, undated (D. Kent Fonner collection); *Cornerstone Clues*, Vol. XX, #1, p. 19.

[11] *Waynesburg Messenger*, 28 January 1863, p. 2.

[12] *Ibid.*

[13] *Ibid.*

[14] An excellent history of the 8th Pennsylvania Reserves is Robert E. Eberly, Jr., *Bouquets from the Cannon's Mouth* (Shippensburg, PA: White Mane Books, 2004). Also see Samuel Bates, *History of Pennsylvania Volunteers*, Vol. I.

[15] Albert Mildred to Nancy Botkins Mildred, 28 August 1861 (letter in private collection of D. Kent Fonner, Beach Lake, PA).

[16] Albert Mildred to Nancy Botkins Mildred, 18 February 1862 (D. Kent Fonner collection).

[17] Diary of Henry Solomon White, 6 February 1862.

[18] *Ibid*, 18 February 1862.

[19] *Ibid*, 7 October 1861.

[20] *Ibid*, 9 October 1861.

[21] *Ibid*, 10 October 1861, 25 October 1861.

[22] *Ibid*, 25 November 1861.

[23] *Ibid*, 15 November 1861.

[24] Diary of Henry Solomon White, 3 February 1862.

[25] *Ibid*, 10 February 1862.

[26] All quotes from the Solomon White Diary on dates designated in text.

[27] Henry Solomon White Diary, 30 November 1861.

[28] *Ibid*, 18 February 1862.

[29] *Ibid*, 14 June 1862 and 15 November 1862.

[30] Letter from S. Hill to Sister, 14 November 1861, *Greene Hills Echo* (Greene County Historical Society: Waynesburg, PA), Vol. 10, #2 (1981), p. 14.

[31] D. S. Hopkins, "Reminiscence of My Service," pp. 16-18.

[32] *Waynesburg Messenger*, 6 November 1861, p. 1.

[33] *Ibid*, 25 December 1861, p. 3.

[34] Diary of Henry Solomon White, 25 December 1861.

[35] D. S. Hopkins, "Reminiscences," p. 16.

[36] Diary of Henry Solomon White, 25 December 1862.

[37] Stewart, pp. 395, 424-429.

[38] Smith, p. 28.

[39] Bates, p. 457.

[40] Stewart, p. 455.

[41] O'Brien, pp. 19-21.

[42] Letter from G. William Pratt to A. L. Myers, 20 November (no year), *Cornerstone Clues*, Vol. XXIV, #1 (February 1999), p. 15.

Home Front Vignette: "A female clad in the uniform . . ."

[The Waynesburg Messenger, on April 13, 1864, reported on an unusual visitor to Greene County. Emma Foster had apparently disguised herself as a man and joined the Union army. Where she came from and where she was headed through Waynesburg remains a mystery. She was, however, an example of the unknown number of women during the Civil War who chose to share the dangers of the battlefield with their husbands, brothers, and fathers.]

"A female clad in the uniform usually furnished by Uncle Sam to his private soldiers, made her appearance in our borough, several days since, and after deceiving our citizens under this guise, the suspicions of some, who are judges of the proportions of the sexes, revealed them to her and she acknowledged that she belonged to that sex usually termed the 'fair sex.' She said her name was Emma Foster, that she had been in the service of the United States, in the Army of the South-west, for nearly three years and had participated in the battle of Chickamauga, and several skirmishes in front of Chattanooga.

Her appearance was that of a youth of twenty summers; but her dialect was that of a sailor who had contended with the storms of the ocean for fifty years. In common parlance she swore like a trooper. This being the first instance of a female attempting to pass for a male, in Waynesburg, of course it created considerable excitement and some conceiving it to be a great misdemeanor, were seriously considering the propriety of having her arrested; but willing that our community should be speedily delivered from the contaminating influence of one who had fallen so far below the virtuous standard of her sex, she was allowed to depart in peace.

Since the foregoing was written we learn that she was arrested in the lower part of the County, upon what specific charge we have not learned, and is now lying in jail."

Chapter VI: "The Falstaff of the Republican"

In the nineteenth century, newspapers made no pretence of objective reporting when it came to political matters. Each local paper during the Civil War era had a clearly defined political view, and Greene County newspapers were no exception. Although very few issues of the *Greene County Republican* from the period are available to researchers, there is no doubt from articles copied by other Pennsylvania papers and comments in local Democrat newspapers that the *Republican* gave full support and endorsement to candidates and policies of that party. The *Waynesburg Messenger* was the Democratic newspaper for the county, and the editors of the two papers continually sparred with each other over national, state, and local issues of the day. By 1860, the *Greene County Republican* was published on a weekly basis under the editorship of Lewis K. Evans, with George A. B. Cooke as printer. When war erupted in 1861, Evans enlisted in Company F, 1st Pennsylvania Cavalry. He was promoted to Second Lieutenant in December 1861. While Evans served with his regiment in Virginia, the paper was managed by Cooke, although Evans' name apparently remained on the masthead as editor.[1] As editor, one correspondent to the *Waynesburg Messenger* noted that Evans "was looked upon as a very clever fellow" who had "many very respectable relatives in the eastern portion of the county."[2]

The *Waynesburg Messenger*, by 1857, was owned and managed by William T. H. Pauley and James S. Jennings. In 1859, Pauley transferred his interest in the paper to James W. Raye who subsequently sold his interest to Waynesburg attorney J. G. Ritche. On August 21, 1861, it was announced that Ritche was leaving the paper and his place would be taken by a new co-editor, Robert W. Jones. Jennings and Jones managed the *Messenger* during the war years. Upon assuming his duties, Jones wrote that he intended the paper to be "dignified and respectful in its tone toward men of all shades and varieties of political opinion, but zealous and decided in its advocacy of the doctrines and policy of the Democratic party as set forth in the 'Cincinnati Platform.'"[3]   In his inaugural editorial, Jones condemned "Fanaticism" of both the North and South. He regretted the current war as "unnatural as it is likely to be sanguinary." He saw termination of the war at the earliest period as the "dictate of wisdom and humanity." Accordingly, he supported the Federal government "in all *proper* and *constitutional* efforts to re-establish its authority and secure a *permanent* and *early* settlement of our present unfortunate sectional differences." He was quick to point out, however, that the paper would continue to hold the Lincoln administration accountable "for any abuse or dangerous and extraordinary exercise of power." Cordial relations with the *Greene County Republican*, however, soon proved to be impossible.

In the late spring of 1862, George Cooke began publishing a series of articles and editorials in the *Republican* attacking the positions of the *Waynesburg Messenger*. Jennings and Jones responded in the *Messenger*, castigating the "brace of editorials in the last Republican" that did the editors "grossest injustice" and that misrepresented their views and position. They wrote that the *Republican* had even questioned their patriotism:

> To reply at length to the misstatements, reflections and uncharitable insinuations of the author would require a degree of forbearance and patience we cannot easily command. We had thought highly of the candor, honesty and manliness of the writer's character as a politician and an opponent, until we read these articles, and the one which preceded them. They have done much to change these impressions, however, and to show us how unfair, ungenerous and unscrupulous partizan bigotry and prejudice may sometimes make an otherwise very clever man and good neighbor.[4]

The editors of the *Messenger* stated that their political opinions were their own and that they were not giving lip service to any party platform which does not "carry the flag and keep step to the music of the Union, and the writer in the *Republican* knows it." For the editors of the *Messenger*, Cooke had become a willful and deliberate falsifier, a sneak, and a coward. "We long since ceased to notice anything appearing in the *Republican*," they wrote, "because it is without a head and is a totally irresponsible sheet." They added that "for nearly a year past its columns have been at the service of every anonymous slanderer who had a load of filth and venom to vomit forth on its readers, and at the mercy of every unfledged scribbler who had brains enough to string together a half dozen sentences of bad English."[5]

Public relations between the two opposing newspapers worsened after L. K. Evans returned as editor of the *Greene County Republican* when he resigned from the army in the summer of 1862. Evans had been born near Garard's Fort in 1831, the son of Evan Evans and Nancy (Myers) Evans. On his mother's side of the family he was a descendant of Reverend John Corbly, who was his great-grandfather. After attending schools in Merritstown and Lewisburg, Pennsylvania, he taught public school for a few years in the late 1850s in Stafford, Ohio. In 1859, Evans became the principal of the Union School in Waynesburg and soon gained an interest in the *Republican*. President Lincoln appointed Evans postmaster of Waynesburg, a position he held until 1865. Evans' first wife, Mary Steele from Stafford, died in 1860, and when the war started, he determined to "resort to that more efficient method of raising recruits for the defense of the land that blessed me, I SET THE EXAMPLE." Evans' resignation from the army coincided with George Cooke's enlistment in Company H, 123rd Pennsylvania Volunteers.[6] Furthermore, George Cooke's father, Joseph Cooke, former owner of the *Waynesburg Eagle*, predecessor to the *Greene County Republican*, and a possible candidate to continue his son's work at the Republican paper, enlisted and served as commissary sergeant in Company A, Eighteenth Pennsylvania Cavalry.[7] The *Messenger* described "the gallant Lieutenant" as "a good-natured, good-hearted, good-for-nothing sort of fellow, fit for chunking holes with 'to keep the wind away.'" They were certain, however, that Evans would be fit "for any *dirty work* his masters [the Republican Party] may have for him to do." Implying that Evans' return from the war to again assume his duties as editor was the result of cowardice following the carnage on the Virginia Peninsula known as the

Seven Days Battles, the *Messenger* reported that Evans *"prudently"* concluded to put a *safe distance* between himself and danger, threw up his commission in *disgust*, and lives to detail his wonderful achievements and 'fight his battles o'er again' to admiring friends and remote posterity."[8] Referring to Evans as the "Falstaff" of the *Republican*, Jennings and Jones reminded their Democratic readers how Evans had joined the "hoss cavalry" the summer before with a "great flourish of trumpets" and how he sent back weekly letters detailing the "prodigious depth of the mud which, from time to time, soiled his theretofore immaculate breeches."[9] A Washington County paper, the *Washington Review*, reminded Editor Jones that Evans had been "among the first to rush to the wars." In 1860, Editor Swan of the *Review* remembered him *"gallantly"* supporting a Wide Awake cape and *charging* with a lamp behind a banner, upon which was inscribed '*down with Union savers.*'"[10]

The *Greene County Republican* retaliated by promoting charges of treason against Democrats in the county, often referring to anyone who opposed any policy of the Lincoln administration as sympathizing with secession and rebellion. As for the *Messenger,* Evans wrote that "loyal men cannot much longer afford to support a disloyal paper. It is enough," he added, "to tolerate it."[11] Taking a cue from other Republican newspapers across the country, Evans began referring to Democrats in the county as "Copperheads." Making light of the matter, the *Waynesburg Messenger* responded that Evans called his opponents "Copperheads" "because we *bite hard*, we presume." For the Democratic paper, moreover, the term offered nothing shameful. After all, according to the Democrat editors, the "Copperhead is a bold, honest snake, and makes an open fight." For them, the copperhead was quite unlike the "Black Snake," which they used as an epithet for Evans and his Republican supporters. The Black Snake, they wrote, "loves secrecy and concealment, and pounces on its victims unawares."[12]

In the pages of the *Republican*, Evans responded by alleging that "shouts we hear for Jeff. Davis, all the threats of resisting the authorities, all the butternut badges that are worn, all encouragement given to the soldiers to desert, in fine all the secret sympathy for the rebels and open treason in our midst, is directly attributable to the teachings of that Copperhead sheet [the *Waynesburg Messenger*]."[13]   On April 29, 1863, the *Waynesburg Messenger* reviewed two years worth of animosity in the county:

> For two years past there has been an impudent and studied effort, on the part of certain Republicans here at Waynesburg to control and direct the course of the "Messenger," to make it swear in their words and support the Administration, right or wrong, and in all its follies and assaults on the rights and liberties of the people. We have been denounced as "Secessionists," threatened with personal violence, and our office with destruction, because we have dared to utter our honest convictions, and have condemned in decided, though in temperate and dignified terms, certain measures of the party in power which we believe and time will show were calculated to defeat the avowed objective of this war,--the preservation of the Government and the restoration of the Union.[14]

Referring to Evans as the "Corporal," the *Messenger* continued to dismiss Evans as "a scurrilous, cowardly, shameless calumniator, the tool and lick-spittle of a profligate clique of 'woolly head' bigots here at Waynesburg, who imported him to bespatter Democrats with his filth and who own and control him as absolutely as if he were their slave."[15]

That summer, after Federal soldiers had been dispatched to Dunkard Township to enforce enrollment for military conscription under the new national Conscription Act, Evans accused the Democratic paper of publishing a "hypocritical article" advising "moderation among the copperheads" of the county. His editorial served only to exacerbate the partisan feelings of the *Messenger* and its Democratic editors. Jennings and Jones accused the Republican press and many Republicans politicians with inciting "riotous demonstrations" throughout the North against Democrats and Democrat newspapers. They stated that letters were sent to the army "intended to inflame the minds of the soldiers" against "prominent Democrats." The result, accordingly, were threatening letters, "paraded with a great flourish of trumpets, in Republican prints," from "deceived and misguided soldiers."[16] An example of some of these letters from Greene County men was a series of letters from a member of Company F, 1st Pennsylvania Cavalry, published in the *Greene County Republican* over the signature "D" and sometimes identified as "Kearny." In one letter, "Kearny" told Republican readers of "his desire that Company F could be back in Greene awhile to suppress the *Messenger*."[17] Democrat Thomas Lucas, Company F, 1st Pennsylvania Cavalry, sent his "compliments to brother D" and asked Jennings and Jones to "tell him that it was very hard when I was at home to stand and hear myself and others stigmatized as being secessionists and traitors to our country." Now, he found the charge "almost beyond endurance" since he had made sacrifice nearly half of his property and "left a home blessed with peace and contentment" to fight a war "brought on by a set of political demagogues, aided and abetted by just such men as him."[18]

Jennings and Jones informed their readers that as "to the threats which have been made against the Messenger and its Editors, we really care no more for them than 'the idle wind that we regard not.'" Believing themselves as patriotic "as any Republican from Maine to Oregon," they declared that they would "not be overawed by such cowardly and disgraceful menaces."[19] In a later editorial, the *Messenger* reminded its readers that L. K. Evans was "a pest and nuisance in the community, and ought to be abated."[20] Eventually, the editors of the *Messenger* refused to even acknowledge the *Greene County Republican*'s attacks. They wrote that "skunk-stirring is always a precarious business."[21] By the fall of 1863, having been advised of further attacks on the paper by Evans in the *Republican*, they simply replied that again, "with a kick, we dismiss the scurvey, up town cur to his kennel."[22]

Regardless of the truthfulness of the charges leveled by each paper against the editors of its competitor, an issue raised is the extent that these vituperative attacks represented underlying tensions between partisans of the two political parties in Greene County. Certainly, elections were hard-fought affairs in Greene County during the war, even though the

Republican Party membership was severely outnumbered. As the war continued, however, the patriotism of 1861 began to give way to a growing discontent by Democrats in Greene County regarding policies pursued by Republicans in the Administration in Washington, D.C. Each side had formulated their own definition of loyalty to the government of the United States as reflected in the bitter struggle waged in the county's weekly newspapers. Any pretence of dispassionate debate over the issues highlighted by the South's rebellion was swept aside in the rhetoric of name-calling and sensational charges of treason leveled by each side against the other. Neither the schoolhouse nor the church was immune from domestic conflict. County School Superintendent, T. J. Teal, reported that the "unsettled conditions of our country created a partisan feeling among both directors and citizens, which destroyed that harmony and hearty co-operation, which is so essential to the prosperity of our free schools."[23] During a school examination at the Albrook School taught by T. Sutton in Centre Township, Reverend William Leonard gave a speech to the parents and school officials in attendance that was reported by a local correspondent as "vile political trash." Reverend Leonard castigated his mostly Democratic listeners for "ignorance and stupidity" and "wickedness and folly" for saying that the Republican administration violated the Constitution. He asserted that one half of those present had never read the Constitution, and the other half did not understand it when they read it. The audience met his remarks with "silent contempt," many leaving the school grounds, including some "prominent members of the Republican party." Reverend Leonard was warned that he "should not take advantage of the pulpit, or school house, to tamper with politics, but should have" his "thoughts fixed on higher objects."[24]

A Wayne Township "Democratic Farmer" wrote to the *Messenger* to berate Reverend Robert Laughlin. Laughlin had published a letter in the *Republican* in which he expressed the need for strong measures to quiet the opposition in Wayne Township to policies of the Lincoln administration. According to "Farmer," Reverend Laughlin:

. . . would imprison, hang and quarter every man living

who dare lift his voice against the extreme fanatical measures of his Abolition brethren and allies, or who dare question the immaculate wisdom of the present Administration in everything they have done, are doing, or may do. He would muzzle the press and put a padlock on every freeman's mouth; and if this wouldn't put a quietus on our protests against converting the War for the Union into a crusade against slavery, he would have his neighbors and Church brethren jibbetted![25]

He went on to say that Reverend Laughlin, who had described himself as part of a "glorious minority" in Wayne Township, had libeled his fellow citizens with charges of "treasonable talk or a treasonable feeling." The partisanship exhibited by the editors of both party newspapers in the county no doubt fueled the bitterness expressed in the community over military conscription and emancipation of slaves in the rebel states.

[1] *Waynesburg Messenger*, 8 January 1862, p. 3.

[2] *Ibid.*

[3] *Ibid,* 21 August 1861, p. 3.

[4] *Ibid,* 28 May 1862, p. 3.

[5] *Ibid,* 21 May 1862, p. 3.

[6] "Death of Well Known Journalist," *Waynesburg Republican,* 18 May 1893; *Waynesburg Messenger,* 26 November 1862, p. 3.

[7] John W. Jordan, LL.D., and James Hadden, editors, *Genealogical and Personal History of Fayette and Greene Counties, Pennsylvania,* Vol. III (New York: Lewis Historical Publishing Company, 1912), 885.

[8] *Waynesburg Messenger,* 30 July 1862, p. 3.

[9] *Ibid,* 6 August 1862, p. 3.

[10] *Ibid,* 13 August 1862, p. 3.

[11] *Ibid,* 3 December 1862, p. 3.

[12] *Ibid,* 25 March 1863, p. 3.

[13] *Greene County Republican* as quoted by the *Waynesburg Messenger*, 22 April 1863, p. 3.

[14] *Waynesburg Messenger*, 29 April 1863, p. 3.

[15] *Ibid*, 22 April 1863, p. 3.

[16] *Waynesburg Messenger*, 27 May 1863, p. 3.

[17] *Ibid,* 18 March 1863, p. 3.

[18] *Ibid,* 5 August 1863, p. 3.

[19] *Ibid,* 27 May 1863, p. 3.

[20] *Ibid*, 10 June 1863, p. 3.

[21] *Ibid.*

[22] *Ibid*, 25 November 1863, p. 3.

[23] *Report of the Superintendent of Common Schools of Pennsylvania for the Year Ending June 1, 1864* (Harrisburg: Singerly & Myers, State Printers, 1865), p. 134.

[24] *Waynesburg Messenger,* 25 March 1863, p. 2.

[25] *Ibid,* 4 March 1863, p. 2.

Chapter VII: ". . . Dunkard Township, the hotbed of copperheadism . . ."

The national military conscription act or draft law passed by Congress on March 3, 1863, was one Republican war measure that met with widespread opposition throughout the North. The law provided that every male citizen of the United States and any foreign born male who had indicated an intent to seek citizenship between the ages of twenty and forty-five was to be enrolled for a draft into military service. A man could avoid being drafted by hiring a substitute to take his place in the army or by paying the government $300 in lieu of a substitute. For those in the North who felt the war should be fought by volunteers, the law was seen as both unconstitutional and a positive infringement upon their freedom. Many Peace Democrats pointed to the provisions regarding the hiring of a substitute as proof that this was "a rich man's war" and "a poor man's fight." Washington Township Democrats in Greene County dismissed Congress' Conscription Act as unconstitutional and "a studied effort to draw a distinction between the rich and the poor."[1] Their resolution also berated the Federal law as "a direct insult to the patriotism of the States."[2]

The editors of the *Waynesburg Messenger* were convinced that the law "confers new and extraordinary powers upon the President:"

> In effect, it establishes martial law over the whole Union. It over rides the constitutional and statute authority of the State Government over their citizens, in respect to military service, and consolidates the supreme power over all things pertaining thereto, in the hands of the President.

They viewed federal conscription as an unnecessary and radical change in the "established Militia System of the country." They noted that the loyal states had already filled, "promptly and patriotically," every requisition for troops made by the federal government so far. "The conscription bill," they warned, "in view of the manifest tendency of the measures of the late Congress toward absolutism, may well excite suspicion and distrust, if not a stronger feeling."[3]

In the heat of July that year, the military draft sparked riots in Boston, Philadelphia, and New York. In New York, the city mob became so violent that Union troops fresh from the battlefield of Gettysburg were sent to quell the disturbance. Peace Democrats sitting as judges in Pennsylvania challenged the draft law at every opportunity. Judge Henry G. Long of Lancaster County, on May 4, 1863, issued a ruling on an application for a writ of habeas corpus by a drafted man named John Shank that since there was no evidence of record that Shank had actually been mustered into service, he could not be arrested as a deserter from the army and was to be discharged from custody.[4] In Schuylkill County, the Court issued bench warrants for the arrest of army personnel who attempted to arrest a drafted man in his home and fired warning shots at him as he fled. The army's provost marshal for the county, C. Tower, noted that "the presiding judge and the two associates of this court all rabidly oppose the war." It was said that the presiding judge "sorrowed publicly over the death of Stonewall Jackson."[5] The Pennsylvania Supreme Court, in the case of *Kneedler v. Lane* (published in volume 45 of the *Pennsylvania Reports* on page 238), issued a preliminary injunction in the fall of 1863, declaring the draft law unconstitutional and directing the army to release any Pennsylvanian in service under its provisions. The preliminary injunction was later dissolved upon a full hearing, but the matter demonstrates the audacity of Peace Democrats like Pennsylvania Justice George W. Woodward when it came to opposition to the conscription act.[6]

Violence against the persons or property of enrollment officers became a common form of resistance to the draft law in some rural counties of Pennsylvania. In a report to the Provost Marshal General of the Army, James B. Fry, dated December 12, 1864, Major Richard I. Dodge, acting provost marshal general for the Western Division of Pennsylvania commented on the difficulties encountered by the army in trying to enforce the draft law in his region. Headquartered in Harrisburg, Major

Dodge called western Pennsylvania "a vast wilderness" with "scarcely any roads." He believed that in the rural areas, the inhabitants were "ignorant and easily imposed upon by designing politicians." As to the great oil region of Pennsylvania, Major Dodge found it "wonderful in its growth and migratory as to its population." Coal miners in western Pennsylvania he thought were "the very worst class of beings, both native and foreign, to be found in this country."[7]

As enrollment for the draft started in Bedford County in June of 1863, Henry Ickes, the enrollment officer in Saint Clair Township, was threatened with "powder and lead." Within a day, his sawmill was burned, causing him $600 in damages.[8] The enrollment officer in Napier Township in the same county had his barn burned.[9] As time went on, it was reported that armed bands of men were accumulating in the woods of Cambria, Center, and Clearfield counties.[10] Reports in Columbia County in 1864 indicated that draft resisters and deserters from the army had accumulated arms and built a fort in Fishing Creek Township which resulted in a military expedition into the region, mass arrests, and the eventual crushing of the movement known as the Fishing Creek Confederacy.[11]

In Greene County, the subject of military conscription was grist for the mill of the Democratic newspaper. When the Commonwealth of Pennsylvania instituted a state draft in 1862 to meet enlistment quotas, the *Waynesburg Messenger* was accused by the Pittsburgh papers of seeking "to make political capital" out of the subject. The *Messenger* claimed that Greene County would be exempt from the draft if given credit for the excess of men in service by counting those residents who had enlisted in regiments outside Pennsylvania:

> Allegany County, it is matter of notoriety, obtained credit for all the men she sent into Virginia and New York regiments, and we are assured Washington County was allowed for all the volunteers she furnished in home and foreign regiments. This was also the case, we presume, in other counties. Why, then, was not Greene County credited for the men she furnished? Was it because of the unfaltering attachment of her people to

the principles and organization of the Democratic Party? We fear it was, and that the facts, when they are developed, as they will be in due season, will confirm this view of the subject.[12]

The editor of the *Pittsburgh Daily Gazette and Advertiser*, however, denied that Allegheny County received any credit for the six hundred men serving in regiments and organizations recruited in other states. To the contrary, he noted that in his order for the state draft, Governor Curtin had specifically stated that "no credit should be allowed for men serving in organizations whose officers had not been commissioned by him." He further chided the Greene County paper for its position:

> But the draft is doubtless "a sore affliction" for certain gentleman whose "attachment to the principles of the Democratic Party" is of a much stronger nature than their attachment to the government which has so summarily "attached" them. The fears of the editor of the *Messenger*, that the draft in Greene County was in punishment for voting the Democratic ticket, are as silly as they are groundless.[13]

The state military draft did cause hardship for some Greene County individuals and families. A drafted man, even in the state draft of 1862, could relieve himself of military obligation if he supplied a substitute. When the draft was conducted in October that year, however, substitutes in Waynesburg were being paid two hundred to five hundred dollars, and they were in demand. The *Waynesburg Messenger* noted the misery brought by the draft to certain families in the county. Stories were rampant of several instances where the draft took away a husband and father who was the sole support of "feeble women and large families of helpless children, leaving them in almost utter destitution or in precarious dependence on the charity of neighbors." It was reported that in one township a man was taken from his family of several little girls and an invalid wife who had not been out of bed for four years except when lifted out by her husband. They owned no real estate and had very little personal property. In another family, a son and two sons-in-law were drafted leaving their wives to care for all their little girls with no male in any household except one boy who was four or five years old.[14] The impact of the draft, moreover, affected the whole community:

> The Draft has been made, and the agricultural and general industrial interests of the county must suffer greatly from the subtraction of a much needed portion of her laboring population. Two-thirds, if not more, of the drafted men were small farmers, unable to buy substitutes, and with families of little children who could be of no service in tilling the soil. The loss of so considerable a number of this class renders the Draft a peculiar hardship in this county.[15]

When the federal government began a military draft in 1863, problems were reported with men being called for military service who were obviously exempt from conscription under the terms of the national law. Some Greene County citizens were enrolled for the draft even though they were missing an arm or a leg. Several men over the age of forty-five and many over the age of thirty-five and married were listed on draft enrollment sheets. All these exempted men, if drafted, had to report to the United States Provost Marshal's office and suffer the expense and loss of time to prove their exemptions under the law.[16] Attorneys in Waynesburg conducted a growing business in assisting drafted men complete the necessary papers for exemption. R. G. Ritchie, R. H. Phelan, G. W. G. Waddell, and D. R. P. Huss all ran articles in the newspaper explaining the exemptions and soliciting those drafted men claiming exemption to use their services. "Drafted men should have their papers properly prepared when they report to the Marshal," warned Attorneys Ritchie and Phelan, "as they will not have time to correct them."[17]

Under the federal military conscription law, Greene County was part of the twenty-fourth district of Pennsylvania when the first enrollment was conducted in June 1863. The district included Greene, Washington, Beaver, and Lawrence counties. The district Provost Marshal's office was located in New Brighton, Pennsylvania, in Beaver County. The Provost Marshal assigned to this district was Captain John Cuthbertson, a combat veteran of Company H of the Ninth Pennsylvania Reserves Infantry. Captain Cuthbertson had been shot through both thighs at the Battle of Fraser's Farm (White Oak Swamp) in Virginia during General McClellan's ill-fated Peninsular Campaign on June 30, 1862. The wounded Cuthbertson was then captured on July 1, 1862 and held in Libby Prison in Richmond until his parole in August that year. After resigning from his command on December 8, 1862, Cuthbertson was appointed Provost Marshal and a member of the board of enrollment for the twenty-fourth district in the spring of 1863.[18] The district enrolling officer was Captain M. R. Adams from Beaver, who had also been wounded in Virginia during the Seven Days Battles while serving in the Tenth Pennsylvania Reserves; and Dr. R. D. Wallace of New Castle served as surgeon for the district Enrolling Board. A detachment of Company F, 16th Veteran Reserve Corps of the United States ("invalid corps") was stationed in a barracks on the corner of Eleventh Street and Fourth Avenue in New Brighton for duty at the Provost Marshal's headquarters.

The enrollment officer for Greene County was William G. W. Day of Waynesburg. Day was the owner of a livery stable and was described as "an excellent fellow" who would "spare no pains to oblige a neighbor."[19] A prominent member of the county's Republican Party, after the war he became owner and editor of *The Waynesburg Republican*.[20] On June 2, 1863, in a letter to the Enrollment Board for the 24th District of Pennsylvania, Day reported that he was "sorry to inform you that the enrollment is not going on pleasantly in Greene County." Unable to find anyone willing to serve as enrollment officer for Dunkard Township, "the hotbed of copperheadism," Day had picked a man he described as very good, "shrewd, calm, and resolute, and a businessman withal" from another township to serve. This man, a Mr. Alexander, had finished his enrollment duties in one township without trouble, but when he traveled into Dunkard Township, he spent a whole day without obtaining one name. Toward evening he entered the general store in Davistown and was met by a large number of men.

These men refused to give him any information, but instead they obtained a rope and threatened to hang him if he did not leave Dunkard Township in three minutes. Mr. Alexander thereupon immediately left the vicinity.

Day wrote that the citizens of Dunkard Township had raised a company to defy Alexander and "just blocked him up so he could not do anything." Day was certain that trouble was brewing in at least three other townships in Greene County. Apparently, the Dunkard Township men argued that there had been an earlier draft made by the state against the township that had never been enforced. It was believed that there were already seven men in the area who had successfully evaded the draft. "Something must be done soon," Day told the Enrollment Board, "or they will have the thing all in their own hands."[21]

Upon receipt of Day's letter, the provost marshal's office in New Brighton, Pennsylvania, in Beaver County, acted immediately and decisively. Deputy Provost Marshal G. S. Baker reported to Washington, D.C. to the provost marshal general, James Fry, on June 6, 1863, that he feared "the trouble" in Dunkard Township was "of some magnitude."[22] On June 5, 1863, Captain Cuthbertson acquired a detachment of twenty-three men from Captain Charles Churchill's Pittsburgh garrison. These men, commanded by a Captain Hays, proceeded to Greensboro with Captain Cuthbertson by steamboat on the Monongahela River. Cuthbertson then led the men by foot over the road from Greensboro to Davistown, taking Mr. Alexander with him. The provost officer tried to conceal his troops' movements, but their slow progress through the hilly Greene County countryside allowed news of their approach to reach Davistown in time for the leaders of the draft resistance in the area to flee.

Mr. Alexander again set up to take the enrollment in Davistown. This time, however, his authority was backed by armed Federal troops under the command of an able officer. The first two men approached by Alexander refused to give their names or ages. Cuthbertson immediately placed them under arrest, and all resistance to the process dissolved, with Davistown residents coming forward voluntarily to give their names. Cuthbertson and his troops remained in Davistown that first night, hoping to catch some of the ringleaders of the resistance. The next day he proceeded to Waynesburg, bringing back a detachment on the following day to Davistown, arriving around midnight. Surrounding the houses of the known leaders of the resistance, Cuthbertson again made an attempt to arrest them. The men were not to be found, however, and Cuthbertson was informed that they had fled to Virginia. In the meantime, Cuthbertson rounded up five deserters in the area along with the two prisoners he had arrested the first day.

The two men arrested the first day for refusing to give their names or ages obtained writs of habeas corpus for their release. A hearing was held before Judge James Lindsey, the Common Pleas Court Judge in Waynesburg, on the validity of the writs. Lindsey, a war Democrat whose brother, William Lindsey, was a captain with the 18th Pennsylvania Cavalry, found to Cuthbertson's satisfaction that refusal to give their names constituted obstruction of an officer performing his duty and the arrests were properly made. Before leaving Greene County, Cuthbertson had Judge Lindsey, James A. J. Buchanan, and other leading citizens of the county, regardless of political affiliation, execute oaths of loyalty to the United States. In his report filed June 12, 1863, Captain Cuthbertson remarked that "War Democrats informed me that the promptness with which a military force had been brought upon the ground of resistance had been attended with happiest results, and that no further trouble need be anticipated."[23]

In the meantime, in Waynesburg, the two political parties sparred over the meaning of it all. Apparently L. K. Evans in an article entitled "Mob Law" in the *Greene County Republican* accused the Democratic newspapers of counseling "resistance to the laws." *The Waynesburg Messenger*, in an article on June 3, 1863, denied any such intent to advise its readers to resist the law. To the contrary, the Democratic paper accused the Republicans of attempting "to stifle Free Speech and muzzle a Free Press . . . ." Such attempts by the Republicans were seen as recognition "of their own shortcomings . . . and the indefensible character of much of their policy and many of their acts."[24]

No matter how events were dissected by the newspapers and politicians, however, one thing is clear about the events in Davistown in the late spring of 1863. This time, there were no reports of warm breakfasts served to wet and hungry soldiers. Captain Cuthbertson, in his report regarding the incident, made no mention of the hospitality of the residents of the village. Federal soldiers and civilians in Davistown this time met as clear adversaries. Captain Cuthbertson's guns had swayed events. Fortunately, the incident and arrests occurred without violence. Resistance to the draft law, however, was a powder keg that only needed the right spark to bring the tragedy of the war closer to the tranquil farm communities of Greene County.

---

[1] *The Waynesburg Messenger*, 6 May 1863, p.1.

[2] *Ibid.*

[3] *Waynesburg Messenger,* 11 March 1863, p. 3.

[4] O.R., Series III, Vol. 3, pp. 244-245.

[5] O.R., Series III, Vol. 3, p. 351.

[6] *Kneedler v. Lane,* 45 PA Reports 238 (PA Supreme Court 1863)

[7] O.R., Series III, Vol. 4, p. 990.

[8] O.R., Series III, Vol. 3, pp. 324-325.

[9] *Ibid,* p. 325.

[10] O.R., Series I, Vol. 43, pt. 2, pp. 525-526.

[11] Turner, pp. 409-470.

[12] *Pittsburgh Daily Gazette and Advertiser*, 4 November 1862, p. 4.

[13] *Ibid.*

[14] *Waynesburg Messenger,* 29 October 1862, p. 3.

[15] *Ibid*

[16] *Ibid,* 12 August 1863, p. 3.

[17] *Ibid,* 22 July 1863, p. 3.

[18] Joseph Henderson Bausman and John Samuel Duss, *History of Beaver County, Pennsylvania, and its centennial celebration* (New York:

Knickerbocker Press, 1904), p. 504; O.R., Series I, Vol. 11, pt. 2, p. 396.

[19] *Waynesburg Messenger,* 7 May 1862, p. 3.

[20] Bates, pp. 657-658.

[21] O.R., Series III, Vol. 3, pp. 321-322.

[22] *Ibid*, p. 321.

[23] *Ibid*, pp. 351-352.

[24] *Waynesburg Messenger*, 3 June 1863, p. 3.

Home Front Vignette: "Fires"

[*One of the origins of the Waynesburg Fire Department can be traced to an article in the Waynesburg Messenger published March 30, 1864. Two fires on the same day threatened to destroy Robert Daugherty's carriage business on Greene Street and the Sheriff's house next to the Greene County Courthouse and Jail. The paper noted the need for the town to provide better fire fighting resources.*]

"Our town had two narrow escapes from destructive fires on the same day during the past week. The first was the carriage manufactory of our excellent friend, Robert Daugherty, which, early discovered, was promptly put out before it fairly got under headway. The second was the sheriff's house, almost adjoining the courthouse and jail. The roof caught from a spark from the chimney, and was fairly in a blaze when first discovered, but was promptly extinguished, with but little damage to the building.

Either of these fires, happening in the night, would have probably resulted in the burning of the buildings, and in the case of the sheriff's house, much other valuable property. We are extremely badly off for the means of extinguishing fires, and these instances should warn us of the necessity of procuring an engine and ladders, and especially should cause the commissioners to have placed on the public square one or two capacious cisterns."

[*A grateful Robert Daugherty published a card of thanks to the citizens of Waynesburg in the same issue of the Messenger.*]

"Messrs. Editors: – Allow me, through the columns of your valuable paper, to return my heartfelt thanks to the citizens of

Waynesburg for their kindness in assisting to put out the fire in my carriage establishment on the morning of the 24th of March. Had it not been for their aid my whole establishment would have been devoured.

Very gratefully yours,
Robert Daugherty."

Chapter VIII: A Murder in Perry Township

      Samuel McCann was a Greene County resident serving with the 7th (West) Virginia Infantry who had returned home to look for deserters. At a bar in Mapletown on Friday, March 14, 1864, McCann attempted to arrest two deserters from the 7th (West) Virginia, James Songston and Otho Herrington. The two men had been missing from the regiment for about a year, and in an article describing the incident in the *Waynesburg Messenger* on March 23, 1864, it was reported that the two had recently returned to Greene County from Ohio where they had enlisted and received bounties. By 1864, this was a common practice for deserters from the army known as "bounty jumping." When McCann found Songston and Herrington in the Mapletown barroom, he immediately accosted them and reached for Songston. Herrington and Songston both drew revolvers, Songston's pistol misfiring just as McCann seized him. Herrington fired his gun at McCann from behind. The bullet passed through the side of McCann's head and came out the corner of one of his eyes. McCann immediately pitched forward into Songston's arms, who then threw him to the floor causing McCann to break his shoulder blade. Songston and Herrington then escaped before any further attempt could be made to arrest them.[1] A Pittsburgh paper noted that the two deserters were later arrested by Captain Coulter, from Greensburg. At that point they were sent to Harrisburg, but they soon escaped. "It is to be hoped," wrote the editor of the *Pittsburgh Gazette,* "that these desperadoes will be apprehended and receive the punishment their crimes so richly merit."[2] The *Messenger* reported that McCann was expected to recover from his wounds.[3]

      On the night of the municipal election in Waynesburg in March 1864, a fight occurred among several young men. One of the crowd was severely cut, and an "outsider," who tried to intervene in the matter was stabbed. The wound was thought to be "dangerous, if not fatal." "The whole affair," noted the *Waynesburg Messenger,* "was most disgraceful to the parties concerned." The editors admonished the Waynesburg "borough authorities to suppress the disorderly demonstrations which have been so common on our streets for a year past, and which may yet result in most serious consequences."[4] A year earlier, in May 1863, a correspondent to the newspaper, identified as "A. Farmer," wanted to know "if the people of Waynesburg approve or countenance dangerous assaults on persons from the country, for no other crime than being Democrats, or expressing their disapproval of the Emancipation Proclamation policy of the Administration, and condemning Abolitionism?" "A. Farmer" informed the residents of Waynesburg that his neighbors would trade elsewhere rather than risk their lives or be subject to assaults for no reason other than their political opinions. Claiming that they were all loyal men, he wrote that they would not subject themselves to "mob law." The editors answered that most citizens of Waynesburg were law abiding and disapproved of the described actions. They reminded "A. Farmer:"

> Our courts are open, and we doubt not, if appealed to, will redress the wrongs complained of by our correspondent, and it would be well if Republicans would leave alleged violations of duty by Democrats to be punished by the legal tribunals of the country. Much of the bad feeling now rife in the land could have been prevented if they had observed the Constitution and laws, instead of resorting to violence and martial law.[5]

Tempers rose at the appearance of a lapel pin made from a copper penny or from a butternut. Many Democrats sported such items on their clothing, not because they necessarily sympathized with the Confederacy, but because their opponents, the Republicans, derisively referred to them as "Copperheads" and "Butternuts." Although some harbored Southern loyalties for one reason or another, most wore the emblems as symbols of pride in their political party. As Jacob Shriver, from Whitely Township, wrote:

> As to the vile aspersion of being a copperhead, all right thinking Democrats will know where I stand by this imputation. I am, as always, a law abiding and

Constitution loving Democrat. There is not a Democrat in the Union who will say that he does not sympathize with the government in any lawful effort to suppress the rebellion; but this is not enough for the negro-worshipers; you must endorse all the unconstitutional acts of the administration now done and to declare in advance your willingness to endorse all asked to be done in the future, or in other words support the administration, not the government.[6]

A subscriber to the *Waynesburg Messenger* wrote about a difficulty which occurred in Newtown, in Whitely Township, on Saturday, July 23, 1863, which started because of the unfortunate attitude of two young men, by the name of Fordyce. One of the boys had just returned from the army, and the two brothers liked to visit Newtown for the purpose of frightening "the Copperheads." One of them even declared "that he could run the damned Copperheads all out of town by exposing to view the mouth of a bottle for a revolver." These comments and similar declarations respecting Democrats had apparently caused some of the young man of Newtown to decide to give these Fordyce boys a demonstration of the law of retaliation by pelting them with rotten eggs. As the subscriber noted:

> If they call us copperheads, they should not attempt to take from us the Copperhead insignia that some of us wear, for the same reason that some men sported a log cabin or hard cider breastpin in the campaign of 1840, because the Democrats called them the log cabin and hard cider boys, and therefore, if we think proper to wear a Copperhead or Butternut breastpin, because Abolitionists call us Copperheads and Butternuts, they have no reason to complain.[7]

The subscriber reminded his readers that all party partisans should take warning from the affair in Newtown. Returning soldiers, home guards, or civilians should all refrain from interfering with the rights of others by using insults, tearing breastpins from their clothing, or assaulting them with rotten eggs. The Fordyce boys, he thought, "were using rotten language, and received a rotten reply." Members of all political parties should avoid any such provocations, since any man looking for a fight usually has an easy time finding one. As he warned:

> If Republicans will allow Democrats to enjoy their opinions and peculiar tastes, I presume there will be no difficulty, but if they persist in using force to compel Democrats to wear what suits their taste, and talk like they talk, and think as they think, the Newtown difficulty will be a small affair in comparison to what will follow such conduct.[8]

This prediction soon proved true at a Democrat meeting held in Carmichaels on August 15, 1863. The meeting progressed quietly, and Republicans attending the gathering respectfully listened to the speakers. At a distance from the street, however, one Democrat supporter was assaulted by a gang of men who ripped his butternut breastpin from his clothes. Friends of the victim soon arrived to his aid, however, and a fight ensued in which revolvers were drawn and three shots were fired. One man by the name of Chambers was shot in the calf of his leg. It was reported that another man, David Hunnel, was shot in the head. It was later learned that instead of being shot, Hunnel had been struck with a drum stick. Republican supporters were warned that the results of the affair could have been much worse, especially since several bystanders also carried revolvers. An unidentified correspondent for the *Waynesburg Messenger* again noted that if the politicians and their supporters "constitute" themselves "rulers of fashion and language and conduct," they "will no doubt involve the community in scenes of riot, bloodshed and murder most foul."[9]

In the late fall of 1864, residents in Springhill Township were startled by news of the violent death of a prominent farmer from the area, Isaac Morford, at Burton Station on the B&O Railroad in West Virginia on November 3rd. Morford and his son, John Morford, had traveled to Burton, about seven miles from their home, to bring over some cattle from his farm near there. While in Burton, they went into one of the stores where they found, among several other local residents, some soldiers, including a Black soldier by the name of Doud. A heated discussion got started about the upcoming Presidential election, and Doud remarked that anyone voting for McClellan was a "d—d ornery man." John Morford stated that he intended to vote for McClellan, and Doud replied "in some insulting language." The two men became embroiled in a heated argument, and an unnamed witness observed Isaac Morford pull out a pistol. In the meantime, Doud and the younger Morford had mutually agreed to drop the subject of the election, and the Morfords left the store for the watering station. A short time later, Doud appeared with two other soldiers and informed John Morford that he had been told about his father's pistol. At that point, Isaac Morford walked up. Doud informed him that he knew about the pistol and he demanded "with an oath" that Isaac surrender it. Before the elder Morford could respond, Doud shot him with his musket, the muzzle being so close that it burned Morford's coat. Morford walked a few steps, fell and died. John Morford having observed his father's shooting, "uttered a severe rebuke to the negro." Doud then tried to run him through with his bayonet. John seized the bayonet with his hand while retrieving a pistol from his own pocket. The three soldiers were beating on him, trying to get him to let go of Doud's bayonet. In the meantime, Morford fired two shots, the last one wounding Doud, but not fatally. At that point, Morford convinced the wounded solder to let him go if he released the bayonet. As soon as Doud had free use of his musket, however, he started to reload. Morford then took off for home, fearing another attack and leaving his father's body and their horses behind. He arrived home sometime after dark. Doud boarded a train coming through and escaped being arrested. One of the other soldiers, named Vanhorn, was arrested at a tavern in Littleton. Isaac Morford's pistol was found in Vanhorn's boot. Isaac Morford's body was brought home to Springhill Township for burial. He was mourned by his wife, several children, and a large circle of relatives and friends.[10]

As the war progressed, Greene County experienced increasing violence. Professor A. J. Waychoff, in his history of Greene County, only relates a single episode of Union soldiers operating in Greene County, describing an incident when

Federal troops camped on the Courthouse lawn and then marched to Mount Morris to break up a band known as the Knights of the Golden Circle.[11]   Exactly what Professor Waychoff was describing is hard to say.   He may have been thinking of some strange combination of the events in Davistown with Captain Showalter and Captain Cuthbertson. It is also possible he was describing a different event altogether. One thing is certain, much more was going on at home during the Civil War era in Greene County than the traditional county historians revealed.

Following the Confederate raid on Morgantown and the B&O Railroad in April 1863, community leaders in Pittsburgh called for the establishment of a telegraph connecting Pittsburgh and Cumberland, Maryland, by way of Washington, Brownsville, Uniontown, and Frostburg, Maryland.   The announced resolution called the proposed telegraph line "a military necessity," and it was noted that branches to Waynesburg and Morgantown were required. *The Waynesburg Messenger* concurred with the proposal.[12] Just when the line was constructed is unclear.   By 1870, however, a Greene County drover named Bear was able to telegraph his bank in Waynesburg to stop payment on a check while he was on business at the East Liberty cattle yards in Pittsburgh;[13] and, by 1873, it was reported that a telegraph line was being built between Waynesburg and Cameron, West Virginia.[14] In 1874, G. Scott Jeffreys held the position of telegrapher in Waynesburg.   He eventually married Lida Culler, the Brownsville telegrapher in 1876.   The couple was married by telegraph, with Jeffreys, Culler, and their wedding party in the Brownsville telegraph office and the minister officiating from the Waynesburg office.[15]

Oil was discovered on Dunkard Creek in 1861, and by 1864, Dunkard Township was in the midst of Greene County's first oil boom.   Oil springs were located at the mouth of Dunkard Creek, and three wells were bored on the Robert Maple farm, two miles upstream. It was noted that the wells were producing five to ten barrels per day of a grade of oil known as "amber." A clear oil not found in other fields in Pennsylvania, it sold at ten cents more per gallon than Venango oil.   One newspaper called Dunkard a "Mecca" for oil developers.[16] A farmer in the region was offered $251,000.00 for his land. The "Kramer" well, which cost less than $10,000, was being offered for sale at $100,000 with an offer of $50,000 on the table.[17] An oil spring was located on the Patrick Donley farm on Dunkard Creek near Mount Morris. By the beginning of 1865, the Dunkard Oil Company had been formed and was advertising the sale of $500,000 capital stock, 100,000 shares at five dollars per share.[18] As one correspondent noted:

> An immense amount of capital has already been attracted here, and the cry is, 'still they come.' New derricks are springing up as if by magic in all directions, and turn your eye in any direction and it will be greeted by the fleecy steam arising from the new diggings.[19]

Farming remained the lifeblood of the county. By 1850, over half the land in the county had been improved for farming. There were more than twice as many sheep in Greene County (55,000) as there were people (22,136 in 1850 and 24,343 in 1860).[20] E. B. Baily, corresponding secretary for the Greene County Agricultural and Manufacturing Society, reported to the Pennsylvania State Agricultural Society that the Greene County organization had held its ninth annual fair at Carmichaels, October 10-11, 1861. The managers had feared that the war would cause the exhibit to be a failure, but Baily reported that "the late fair was scarcely second, in the number and quality of the articles on exhibition, to any of its predecessors."[21] Morgen R. Wise predicted for the *Greene County Republican* that ". . . Greene County will be one of the foremost wool growing districts in the State . . . ." He believed that in 1861, "the clip has been improved at least fifty per cent, both in quality and condition."[22] In the *Waynesburg Messenger*, Wise summarized the wool growing efforts of several Greene County farmers:

> We notice that a number of farmers have succeeded in so crossing and selecting their stock that the quantity and quality of their fleeces is of such grade that it is highly commendable. Of these, we think Mr. Dennis Iams stands among the first rank, as he has spent almost a lifetime in this laudable enterprise of improving

sheep. Also, we think Mr. Timothy Ross deserves notice as a wool grower, judging from the fancy lot of wool we bought of himself and Mr. Longdon; knowing that he has spared neither pains or expense in selecting from the best flock in his vicinity which is noted for fancy wools.[23]

"To venture a prediction," noted Wise, "we have full assurance that Greene County will be one of the foremost wool growing districts in the State . . . ."[24] As early as 1853, the Pittsburgh papers reported that a Greene County merino ram had sold for $500.00.[25] Ten years later, a Washington Township farmer, Samuel Braden, received first premium on Spanish merino sheep at the Indiana State Fair.[26] The growing importance of sheep in Greene County was emphasized when the *Waynesburg Messenger,* on December 11, 1861, along with politics and news of the war, included an article of interest to a vast number of the county's farmers on "Destruction of sheep by dogs."

T. W. Taylor reported that on three successive nights in November, dogs attacked sheep in Washington Township on farms near the Washington County border. One hundred and thirty-seven sheep were killed or wounded. Forty-two of the sheep, owned by Samuel Braden and Adney Lacock were valued at three dollars per head. Hiram Swart lost fifty from his flock worth four dollars per head, and the remaining sheep, including some Merino rams, had been owned by Robert Bristor. Bristor's loss was calculated at five dollars per head. Four of the offending dogs were found in the fields and immediately killed.[27]

Although stock raising remained the main emphasis of Greene County farmers, there were some areas of the county quite suitable for crops. Morgan Bell, from Morgan Township, developed a specimen of wheat on his farm which he named "McClellan Wheat." "It excels, in size and plumpness," described the *Waynesburg Messenger,* "anything we have seen." On John B. Gordon's farm in Franklin Township, that summer, it was reported that three and a half bushels of a strain of wheat called Carmack and Turkish Flint was sowed. The yield proved to be one hundred and forty bushels.[28]

On November 20, 1864, a woman from Richhill Township, identified only by the initials M. L. R. wrote a letter to "Cousin Neddy." From her point of view, despite the tragedy of the war, farmers in Greene County were doing well. She wrote:

> ... everything appears to be plenty, and demands a high price, cattle is worth Seven cts [per pound or seven dollars per hundred-weight] in the rough (fat cattle) hogs, 10 to 12, do. Sheep Six dollars per head, and upwards, Chickens 50 [cents] per pair, and everything in proportion, yet there appears to be plenty of everything, and that is good, I suppose one reason of the high prices of everything is money being so plenty, everybody is into Some kind of speculation, Some in oil, some in western cattle and hogs, Some one thing and some another . . . .[29]

She also told Cousin Neddy that "Joe" had purchased some cattle and hogs "out West this fall." She hoped that the venture would turn out well and that Joe would "make considerable on them, enough to hire him a Substitute, for I expect there will be another big draft this winter, or next spring." "Their [sic] is some Soldiers here at Waynesburgh," she wrote, "They are part of an Invalid Corps, they are taking deserters, etc etc . . . ."[30]

The soldiers stationed in Waynesburg were Company F, 16th Regiment of the Veteran Reserve Corps, commanded by Captain N. H. Randlett. The military force had been sent to Greene County in early October. The *Waynesburg Messenger* reported:

> We were not a little surprised to learn a few days ago, that a company of soldiers was on its way to Greene county. Why they were sent here we know not, nor at whose instance; the public knows no reasons for their presence. Perhaps our valiant Provost Marshal knows something about it. His *unwillingness,* personally, to discharge the duties devolving upon him in reference to the draft, and his uniform practice of devolving upon others the duties which belong to

himself, would seem to account for the presence of the military force.[31]

The newspaper noted the "uniform good behavior and courtesy" of the soldiers, "The true soldier is always a gentleman, and such we find those quartered among us to be."[32]

Among the deserters being sought by the Federal authorities in early November 1864 was a young man from Perry Township named Thomas Phillips. Phillips, who was about thirty years old at the time, was the son of Peter Phillips, a Perry Township farmer who according to the 1860 census owned property worth about $300. Having been drafted into the military in the summer of 1863, the younger Phillips failed to report and made it well known in the community that he was not going to report. Phillips was not alone in his determination. According to statistics released by U. S. Provost Marshal Cuthbertson for the 1863 draft, nearly two hundred men in the Twenty-fourth District failed to report. It was noted that 3,993 men had been called in the draft that summer. Of this number, 1,104 paid the necessary commutation to be released from service. Two hundred and thirty-one were mustered into the army, and one hundred and sixty-seven provided substitutes, who presumably were also mustered into service. One hundred and seventy-one failed to report. The remaining men on the list were exempted for one reason or another.[33]

On Sunday evening, November 6, 1864, Phillips was attending a party in Perry Township when he was informed that Federal authorities were on their way to take him into custody. He immediately left the party, declaring his intention to shoot anyone who tried to arrest him. Apparently deciding to ambush his pursuers, Phillips concealed himself along the road. Not long after that, William Brown, a son of Reuben Brown, Jr., a prominent farmer in Perry Township, and T. S. Morris, a son of Mount Morris merchant E. F. Morris, came along the road on their way home from a wedding. When they approached the place where Phillips was hiding, he fired at them three times, missing Morris but hitting William Brown with the second shot in the left temple.[34]

Two days later, on November 8, 1864, E. F. Morris appeared before Perry Township Justice of the Peace A. F.

Ammons and swore out an affidavit for Thomas Phillips' arrest on the charge of assault with intent to kill T. S. Morris and William Brown, Brown having so far survived his wound. The township constable, Brice Howard, arrested Phillips, who was then released on bail set at $3000. At that time a Charles Coss and William Phillips put up the money for bail.

Dr. L. W. Ross was called to attend Brown's wound. The doctor was able to remove some bone fragments from Brown's brain, but he could not locate the ball, which he believed had lodged against the opposite side of the skull. Within a few days, William Brown died, and his father, Reuben Brown, Jr., appeared before Justice of the Peace Joseph Connor in Mount Morris to swear an affidavit for an arrest warrant for Thomas Phillips for murder. Justice Conner issued a warrant, and Constable Brice Howard again took Phillips into custody, committing him to the county jail in Waynesburg on November 12, 1864. The Washington *Reporter and Tribune* noted in an article published November 16, 1864, that Phillips may have shot Brown "perhaps thinking" he and Morris "were the parties in pursuit of him." Phillips, Brown, and Morris had all been friendly with each other, so no other motive could be given. At any rate, tempers in Perry Township were running high. It was reported that threats had been made to lynch Phillips before he was arrested and jailed.[35]

The case of *Commonwealth of Pennsylvania v. Thomas Phillips* was filed in the Court of Quarter Sessions of Greene County at number 7 December Sessions 1864. The county district attorney, J. G. Ritchie, sought an indictment for "murder felony" from the Grand Jury. The Grand Jury listened to testimony from several witnesses, including Thaddeus S. Morris, Dr. Spencer Morris, Dr. L. W. Ross, Washington Fox, Phillip Heite, Mary Phillips, Charles Coss, John Coss, Brice Howard, Minor Long, Cisey Rose, Ellsworth Russell, and John McClure. After due deliberation under their foreman, W. S. Ritchie, the Greene County Grand Jury returned a verdict of "ignoramus" in the case filed against Thomas Phillips. A Latin term literally meaning, "We do not know," the verdict of "ignoramus" was a decision by the Grand Jury rejecting the indictment. In essence, the jury decided that even if the facts in the bill of indictment drawn by the district attorney were true,

Phillips' conduct did not warrant criminal punishment. Phillips, however, was apparently turned over to the Provost Marshal and mustered into the army in December 1864.[36]

As frustrating as the verdict must have been for the Reuben Brown family, it is just as puzzling for anyone looking at the case in hindsight. The only documents available in the Greene County Clerk of Court's Office are the entries in the Quarter Sessions docket, the affidavits for the arrest warrants, the warrants themselves, a transcript from Justice of the Peace Ammons docket, and the indictment. There is no transcript of testimony, so it is hard to analyze what happened. The surviving records seem clear that Thomas Phillips did shoot William Brown that night on November 6, 1864. Indeed, the Brown family was convinced of it because in Bates' biographical sketch of Reuben Brown, Jr., he states that Reuben's son William was killed by accident by a deserter during the Civil War.[37] Calling the incident an "accident" may be the key to understanding the verdict. It is possible that the jury looked at the case as a tragedy for both the Brown and the Phillips families. William Brown had been killed by mistake. Thomas Phillips, because of a military draft law passed by a distant government in Washington, D.C., had felt it necessary to defend himself from what several citizens of the county no doubt believed would be an illegal arrest for violating an unconstitutional law.

If this analysis is close to the truth, then the jury may simply have decided to deal with Brown's death by leaving the parties in the position they occupied by virtue of the tragedy of the times. Recognizing that the shooting was really only an accident, the jury simply could not bring themselves to find enough evidence to indict Thomas Phillips for an intentional killing. Civil war violence in Greene County, in Perry Township in 1864 as in Dodysburg in 1859, did not come in the form of battle or soldiers firing on civilians. More tragically, it came to the community in the experience of the senseless horror of neighbor killing neighbor.

---

[1] *Waynesburg Messenger*, 23 March 1864, p. 3.

[2] *Pittsburgh Daily Gazette and Advertiser*, 7 May 1864, p. 3.

[3] *Waynesburg Messenger*, 23 March 1864, p. 3.

[4] *Ibid,* 16 March 1864, p. 3.

[5] *Ibid,* 27 May 1863, p. 3.

[6] *Ibid,* 25 May 1864, p. 2.

[7] *Ibid,* 19 August 1863, p. 2.

[8] *Ibid.*

[9] *Ibid,* 26 August 1863, p. 2.

[10] *Ibid,* 9 November 1864, p. 3.

[11] Waychoff, p. 50.

[12] *The Waynesburg Messenger*, 20 May 1863, p. 3.

[13] *Lehigh Register*, 9 November 1870, p. 1.

[14] *Beaver Radical*, 7 March 1873.

[15] Western Union Telegraph Company, *Journal of the Telegraph* (New York), Vol. 7, No. 7, p. 106. Mr. and Mrs. Jeffreys wedding is described in Thomas C. Jepsen, *My Sisters Telegraphic: Women in the Telegraph Office, 1846-1950* (Athens, Ohio: Ohio University Press, 2000), p. 137.

[16] *Columbia Spy* (Columbia, PA) 26 November 1864, p. 2. For more detail regarding oil developments, see D. Kent Fonner, "A Brief History of Oil and Gas Development in Greene County, Pennsylvania (1861-1930)," (manuscript in collection of Cornerstone Genealogical Society, Waynesburg, PA, dated 2000), pp. 8-10; also see *Waynesburg Messenger*, 13 March 1861, p. 2; *Daily Evening Bulletin* (Philadelphia, PA), 9 June 1864, p. 8; Ibid, 8 December 1864, p. 1; *Lancaster Intelligencer*, 28 June 1865, p. 2.

[17] *Daily Evening Bulletin*, 8 December 1864, p. 1; *Columbia Spy*, 26 November 1864, p. 2.

[18] *The Press* (Philadelphia), 4 January 1865, p. 3.

[19] *Columbia Spy*, 26 November 1864, p. 2.

[20] Smith, pp. 30-31.

[21] *Report of the Transactions of the Pennsylvania State Agricultural Society*

for the Years 1861-'62-'63, Vol. VI (Harrisburg, PA: Singerly & Meyers, State Printers, 1863), p. 685.

[22] *Greene County Republican,* 8 October 1861, as quoted by Powell, p. 79.

[23] *Waynesburg Messenger,* 16 October 1861, p. 3.

[24] *Ibid.*

[25] *Daily Morning Post* (Pittsburgh), 21 July 1853, p. 2.

[26] *Waynesburg Messenger,* 28 October 1863, p. 3.

[27] *Waynesburg Messenger,* 11 December 1861, p. 3.

[28] *Ibid,* 15 July 1863, p. 3.

[29] Photocopy of Letter from MLR to Cousin Neddy, dated from "Rich Hills" 20 November 1864 (original in possession of Dr. Thomas Pavick, Waynesburg College, Waynesburg, PA).

[30] Ibid.

[31] *Waynesburg Messenger,* 5 October 1864, p. 3.

[32] *Ibid.*

[33] *Ibid,* 27 January 1864, p. 3.

[34] Documents and information relating to the case of *Commonwealth of Pennsylvania v. Thomas Phillips* are at #7 December Sessions 1864, Greene County Clerk of Court's Office, Greene County Courthouse, Waynesburg, PA.

[35] *The Reporter and Tribune* (Washington, PA), 16 November 1864, p. 3; *Waynesburg Messenger,* 16 November 1864, p. 3.

[36] Bausman and Duss, p. 602.

[37] Bates, p. 813.

Chapter IX: "To Intimidate the Disaffected"

By the fall of 1864, the *Greene County Republican* reported that "long talked of draft resistance" was being "inaugurated." Government agents had spent a mid-September day in Whitely Township serving draft notices on various men in the area. In the evening, they put up for the night at the home of Lisbon Staggers. That night someone, described by the newspaper as "poltroons and miscreants," made their way into the stable and shredded their saddles and bridles. In addition, they stole the agents' horses, mutilating them "in a barbarous and most shocking manner." When the horses were recovered, it was discovered that whoever perpetrated the theft had shaved off their manes and cut off the poor animals' tails and ears. The editor condemned this brutality with a stinging attack:

> This, then, is the kind of warfare for which they have made such great preparations and of which they have boasted so much--a warfare on dumb brutes--the work of cowards and dastards, too base and niggardly to be called vandalism. The assassin, the cut-throat and the land-pirates are gentleman to these miserable wretches. Rebels in arms spurn to stoop to such mean, contemptible outrages. It is left for the copperhead sneaks to be guilty of perpetrating this crowning deed of infamy. And yet they are good McClellan men! Loyal peace shrieker's! "Constitutional" Democrats![1]

Although it has become fashionable for historians to attack Abraham Lincoln on the basis of his policies regarding martial law, enforcement of the draft law, and suspension of the writ of habeas corpus, the fact remains that he and his advisors maintained enough faith in American democracy to allow the existence of a "loyal opposition" in the North and to permit the election process to continue even in the darkest periods of the war. For all the talk by Democrats in the North of "American Bastilles," a name given to military prisons holding civilians arrested by the military on one charge or another, the northern states did not experience the slaughter of political opponents that other republics have experienced during similar crises.

Since Pennsylvania was a key state in national and presidential politics, it is understandable that the Republicans paid close attention to antiwar movements there and the actions and words of the Democratic leaders throughout the Commonwealth.

The race for governor in Pennsylvania in 1863 was extremely important to Lincoln. Republican Governor Andrew J. Curtin had proven to be a strong supporter of the war effort. His opponent, Peace Democrat George W. Woodward was a Pennsylvania Supreme Court Justice who supported the preliminary injunction against enforcement of the draft law in Pennsylvania issued in the case of *Kneedler v. Lane*. The election could therefore be viewed as a referendum on the Republican Party's execution of the war. If Curtin lost his bid for reelection in 1863, there was a chance that Lincoln would lose the state and reelection as President in 1864. In analyzing Pennsylvania politics for President Lincoln in a letter dated June 17, 1863, Senator Edgar Cowan informed Lincoln that the voters of Pennsylvania "constitute but two great parties, Democratic and Whig, just as they did 20 years ago—and the nature of men out of which these parties grew remains the same." He remarked that half of the people, representing the Democratic Party, "are bitterly opposed . . . nay they hate and abhor . . . abolitionists." Of the Republicans in Pennsylvania, he estimated that nine-tenths were opposed to the radical policies of the abolitionist wing of the party. Yet, Senator Cowan warned Lincoln "many now believe that the War is now really waged for the sake of Abolitionism and not to restore the Union."[2] As the gubernatorial election approached in Pennsylvania, Andrew Curtin informed Lincoln on September 4, 1863, if the election were held that day "the result would be extremely doubtful." "In the cities and towns," Curtin continued, "the changes are all in our favor, but in the country, removed from the centers of intelligence, the Democratic leaders have succeeded in creating prejudice and passion, and have infused their poison into the minds of the people to a very large extent, and the changes are against us."[3] Despite his pessimism in September, Curtin won reelection as governor of Pennsylvania when the general election was held in October. In Greene County, however, Curtin was defeated by a margin of two to one, with 2960 votes cast for Woodward and 1484 votes for Curtin.[4]

By mid-1863, unionists throughout Pennsylvania and the North had begun to form political societies known as Union Leagues for the purpose of more effectively opposing southern sympathizers. Believing that the copperheads, as they were known, were organized in vast secret organizations like the Knights of the Golden Circle and the Order of American Knights, the Union Leagues took measures to insure the propagation of pro-union literature and speakers to support the war effort. Basically an auxiliary of the Republican Party, the Union Leagues eventually led to the formation in several states of a Union Party, a bipartisan political party composed of moderate Republicans and war Democrats. As the war continued, Republican Party strength in Greene County remained weak. Following the 1862 township elections in March, a Morgan Township correspondent to the *Waynesburg Messenger* reported the entire success of the Democratic ticket in that municipality. "The test candidates of both parties were first-rate men," he noted, "and the Republicans were defeated only because they were Republicans."[5] That summer, the newspaper described a Republican Party meeting at the courthouse as a "small gathering of the 'faithful few' who still cling to the fortunes of this doomed, if not already obsolete party." Only fifteen or twenty adults participated in a vote taken during the course of the meeting. Party leaders present included R. W. Downey, who gave a speech while a committee composed of John H. Wells, Ezra M. Sayers, and James Throckmorton met to draft resolutions. The meeting was also addressed by Washington County Republican George V. Lawrence.[6] Another Republican county meeting in August that year was attended by only twelve "full-grown delegates."[7]

"Union Leagues" began appearing in various Greene County townships during the spring of 1863. The *Messenger* warned county Democrats to be on their guard against "the Abolitionist demagogues and office-hunters who would seduce them into" joining a "dangerous organization."[8] According to an earlier report, the editors noted that "the new-fangled 'Union League' party is only Republicanism revamped."[9] Dr. Alexander Patton wrote from Harrisburg that the Union Leagues were "a sequel to Knownothingism, intended to

133

deceive." He believed they were "headed by the most loathsome, besotted, and bigoted politicians of the radical Republican school." "These men care nothing about the Union of our Fathers," Patton opined, "they have for their pole star filthy lucre, negro love, and continuance in place."[10] The Democrat newspaper in Waynesburg denounced the *Greene County Republican*'s call for a "Union Mass Meeting" in Waynesburg for Saturday, April 18, 1863, as being "made at the instance of a few Abolition leaders and wire-pullers here at Waynesburg who are anxious to ventilate their rusty and 'shocking bad' oratory and make a little capital for their sinking party." Democrats were warned to avoid the meeting, and any who attended could expect "an elegant opportunity to throw themselves, body and breeches, into the arms of Black Republicanism."[11] One Democratic leader, who became deeply involved in the county's Union Leagues, and later the Union Party, was J. A. J. Buchanan. Buchanan was a featured speaker at the mass meeting on April 18, and he became a frequent speaker at Union Party meetings throughout the county until the end of the war.[12]

At the mass Union meeting held in Waynesburg that April, Buchanan was praised by the *Greene County Republican* for a "speech at once logical, convincing, incontrovertible, and fearless—a speech condemning the copperheads and urging them to leave off their crusade against the Government."[13] In a letter to the *Messenger,* in which Buchanan defended himself against charges of disloyalty to the Democratic Party, he stated his position on the conduct of the war against the rebellion from the standpoint of a "Union Democrat:"

> They believe the Government must be supported whilst it yields us protection.
> They believe that Government consists in the Constitution and the laws.
> And that no policy of any officer of the Government will form a sufficient cause to resist the one or infract the other.
> That when a law has been enacted, be it ever so oppressive, the people have no alternative but an appeal to the Courts to stay the evil.

That the ballot box is the only proper remedy for the encroachment of power, and it is the bounden duty of the citizen to obey until the remedy can be legally claimed.

They believe the army of the United States has been legally called into action, and are fighting for the Constitution and the Union, and not a "mob" convened to fight against the same.[14]

He further castigated those in the Greene County Democrat organization who condemned himself and other county Democrats, including Abel Carey, J. Randolph Hewitt, John Munnell, and Andrew Wilson, Jr., for holding to such principles and accusing them of being traitors to the party. Buchanan did not agree with every war policy of the Lincoln administration. He believed the President's suspension of the writ of *habeas corpus* was "doubtful" under the Constitution; but, in the absence of any Supreme Court decision regarding the matter, he thought Lincoln "entirely justified in exercising it whenever the necessity might arise in favor of the general necessity" of suppression of the southern rebellion. He believed that the military conscription law passed by Congress was constitutional. Lincoln's emancipation policy, however, he opposed as being "impolitic," although he admitted that "if he were the President, he would do just as he pleased" regarding the emancipation issue. He conceded that Lincoln possessed full information respecting the view of foreign powers and may have been compelled to issue the Emancipation Proclamation to stop English and French intervention in the war in favor of the South.[15]

The *Waynesburg Messenger* argued that Buchanan's speech, regardless of his intentions or expectations, was "favorable" to the Republican Party. The editors questioned Buchanan's adherence to "Democratic" principles when he raised issues about "the loyalty and patriotism of his party," or joins "in the hue and cry of the opposition that all Democrats are 'traitors' and 'secessionists' who do not swear in their words, or who do not give an unquestioning support to every act of the Administration, politic or impolitic, constitutional or unconstitutional." For Jennings and Jones, Buchanan's

135

acceptance of the name, "Union Democrat," impugned the Unionism of other Democrats who failed to "follow his lead, hold to his views, or who do not enjoy as large a degree of Republican favor as he has the good fortune to possess."[16]

In May, 1863, William A. Porter, a Waynesburg merchant, had the privilege to speak to the Union League of Philadelphia. *The Press* of Philadelphia noted that Porter "delivered a spirited and patriotic address." Porter was described as a "Democrat of long standing" who was "most ardently and fervidly attached to the Union cause, and resolutely in favor of the war for the crushing out of the rebellion." In his speech, Porter described his experience when he recently spoke to the Democratic Central Club. Apparently, Porter caused a sensation with his fellow state Democrats when he stated that he was a "fighting Democrat, and, for one, determined to support the Administration in its efforts to suppress the rebellion." He further declared that he would never allow himself to be called a "Copperhead." At that, a number of his audience rose to their feet and began shouting him down, declaring, "We are Copperheads!" Some called for the speaker to be ousted from the hall. Porter told the Philadelphia Union League that his voice was drowned out in the bedlam and he was forced to retire.[17]

Following his speech to the Philadelphia Unionists, Democrats in Greene County began circulating rumors that Porter had "renounced" his "allegiance to the Democratic party, and joined the '*Union Leaguers.*'" In June, Porter wrote a letter to the *Waynesburg Messenger* in which he affirmed that despite the rumors he was still a Democrat "in thought, word and deed." He dismissed the Union Leagues as "secret political organizations, which, in my judgment, are as adverse to truth and good morals, as they are destructive of the liberties of the people." Porter stated that his intent was "to adhere to the Democratic organization so long as it remains true to its past history, and loyal to the Constitution and laws . . . ." As to the issue of civil war, however, he firmly stated that he was "for supporting the Government, enforcing its laws, crushing the Rebellion and sustaining our heroic soldiers in the field."[18]

As the autumn state elections approached in 1863, The *Waynesburg Messenger* remarked in bold type that "POLITICS

MAKE STRANGE BED FELLOWS." Stating to its readers that "this old saw" was being proven "in this locality," the editors advised that "several fallen Democrats are 'bunking' with [E. M.] Sayers, [Alfred] Myers and others of their ilk [leading Greene County Republicans], and laboring hand in hand with them for the spread of Abolitionism." The Democratic newspaper could not help but "wonder how they feel 'down there.'"[19] The *Greene County Republican,* however, proudly proclaimed, after the victory of Governor Curtin, "Abandoning the organization of the spurious Democracy," J. A. J. Buchanan, "took a bold stand in favor of the Union candidates, and by reason of his eloquence and influence contributed as much as any one man to the reelection of Andrew G. Curtin." L. K. Evans was certain that Buchanan's labors had reduced the Democrat majority in Greene County from more than two thousand to less than fifteen hundred.[20]

The Union Party had a more difficult time in the state senate election that year. In western Pennsylvania, Greene and Washington county unionists met to discuss possible candidates. John C. Flenniken, chairman of the Union Senatorial Conferees, drafted a letter on September 21, 1863, to former Greene County Sheriff and Prothonotary, John Lindsey. Lindsey was the father of Judge James Lindsey of Greene County, and a long-time leader of the county's Democratic Party. Flenniken informed Mr. Lindsey that at the conferees' meeting at Prosperity on September 11, 1863, Lindsey was nominated as the candidate of the local Union Party for election to the Pennsylvania State Senate. "Many of your fellow citizens," wrote Flenniken, "anxiously await your acceptance of this nomination."[21]

In the meantime, western Pennsylvania Democrats organized their state senate campaign by nominating Colonel William Hopkins of Washington County.[22] Hopkins was described as "an old political sinner of fair exterior" who "will bring more legislative experience to the Senate than is possessed by any other member of that body." Having served a previous term as Speaker of the state assembly in 1838 and Canal Commissioner in 1852, Hopkins was a current member of the Assembly from Washington County.[23] One "active Democrat" in Greene County told the Harrisburg *Daily Patriot and Union* that "we have excellent district and county tickets," and, "you may expect a good account of us, on the second Tuesday of October next, if the Czar [President Lincoln] graciously permit us to hold an election on that day."[24]

Describing an "active contest" for the state senate position in Washington and Greene Counties, the *Evening Telegraph* from Harrisburg reported that in the general election in 1862, the two southwestern Pennsylvania counties "gave a heavy Democratic majority." "Strong hopes," continued the editor, "are now entertained of the election of Mr. Lindsey."[25]

From his home in Greene County, however, "the venerable John Lindsey" felt compelled to decline the Union Party nomination for the state senate. His son, Captain William C. Lindsey, had been killed, July 6, 1863, while leading a mounted charge by two battalions of the 18th Pennsylvania Cavalry against the rear guard of Robert E. Lee's Army of Northern Virginia at Hagerstown, Maryland.[26] Mr. Lindsey explained his position regarding the nomination:

> "I am growing old, my health is very feeble, and a recent domestic bereavement has fallen with sorrowful weight upon me, and upon my family, and I have now neither heart nor strength for the strife of a political campaign."[27]

To quiet any doubts about his views, nevertheless, Lindsey added that, although he remained a Democrat, "I am now, as ever, earnestly in favor of a vigorous prosecution of the war for the suppression of the atrocious and accursed Southern rebellion; and what little I have of life and strength is devoted to the cause of the Union of these states."[28]

John Lindsey having refused the nomination, the Union Party settled on John C. Flenniken as its candidate for the state senate. Flenniken was described by his opponents as a "very clever, sensible, and upright man," but for at least two years he had become "a Republican of the strictest acct."[29] When the votes were counted for the state senate seat in October, William Hopkins won. The election results, however, were closer than the Peace Democrats in the region would have wished. "He comes to the Senate," reported the *Franklin Repository*, "with a popular majority against him of over 200 in his own county and less than the party vote in Green[e]." The Chambersburg paper dismissed Hopkins as "a bitter narrow Democratic partisan . . . ."[30]

The *Greene County Republican* endorsed Lincoln for reelection as President as early as October 1863.[31] County Democrats endorsed the nomination of Major General George B. McClellan; and the party leaders from at least one township, Perry, called for the county organization to support the nomination of a "Peace Democrat."[32] Lincoln won Pennsylvania in the presidential election in 1864, although Greene County was one of twelve Pennsylvania counties that voted against him. The county's dissatisfaction with the Lincoln administration's war policies was expressed by her soldiers in the field. Letters home bitterly complained about the Emancipation Proclamation as early as the winter of 1863. An unnamed member of the 8th Pennsylvania Reserves expressed his bitterness toward abolitionists to the *Waynesburg Messenger*'s readers:

> The people at home don't know what is good for themselves, especially the Abolitionists. I could shoot one of them as quick as I would a rebel, and think I was doing my country a good turn. This is what all say here.[33]

Thomas J. R. Fry, of the 85th Pennsylvania Regiment, wrote from South Carolina that when he enlisted he was a Republican, but now, in March 1863, he was a Democrat. He denounced the war as being fought solely for the freedom of Blacks, and he complained that "contrabands" were being treated better by the army than private soldiers.[34]

As the Presidential election year of 1864 opened, a Private in Company A, 140th Pennsylvania Volunteers, complained that nothing "but lying Abolition journals can now find access to our Camp." He condemned the way that shortly after his enlistment "the whole policy of the Administration was changed, and the war was made a crusade against slavery, and against the lives and property of private citizens." Moreover, he bitterly described the treatment he and his comrades suffered for their opinions about "the extreme radical policy of the President:"

Now, if I refer to the perjury and corruption of the Administration, in common conversation, I, and all those who think with me, are denounced as "copperheads," "secesh," "traitors," etc., etc. Ye Gods! Who can endure all this? Separated from friends and home, enduring all the toils and hardships of a soldier's life, facing the belching cannon upon more than one hard-fought field—am I to be denounced as a traitor, merely because I do not blindly and implicitly endorse the negro policy of the Administration? Can flesh and blood stand this?[35]

A straw vote of Company A, 140th Pennsylvania, made in April 1864, resulted in forty-six votes for Democrat, Major-General George B. McClellan, and fifteen votes for Lincoln.[36] A month later, several members of Company A, including Sergeant Mark G. Spragg, Corporal Charles T. Hedge, Commissary J. S. Herrington, and Privates George W. Wilson, Benjamin Dunston, David Frays, George Freeland, Origon T. Walters, Job Smith, Ehud Steele, J. R. M. Green, Samuel Roupe, and William Ogden, sent a letter to the *Messenger* stating their support for the newspaper and letting the people of "Little Greene" know that they were still Democrats. They believed Company A was "almost unanimous" for McClellan and that there were not "more than six or eight negro worshippers in our company." "All the soldiers ask is a chance to pay Old Abe off for trying to make a nigger equal to a white man," they stated, "and if you will nominate Gen. George B. McClellan, the soldiers will give him two votes where they give Old Abe one."[37] When a similar straw vote was held in the Eighteenth Pennsylvania Cavalry in September 1864, only three Greene County men from Company A stepped out to support Lincoln, while thirty-nine voted for McClellan with a loud cheer. The polling results of the whole brigade to which the Eighteenth Pennsylvania Cavalry was attached, however, indicated a three to one majority for Lincoln.[38] One Greene County soldier who supported Lincoln, Isaac W. Scherich, of the Eighteenth Pennsylvania Cavalry, had an interesting experience when he came home on furlough to vote for the President's reelection. Scherich had been wounded during a charge against a Confederate position in the Shenandoah Valley, Virginia, on September 19, 1864. The ball shattered his arm above the elbow. Eventually, a surgeon of the First Vermont Cavalry, named Ames, amputated the arm. By October 22, Scherich was in a military hospital in Wilmington, Delaware. He received a twenty-day furlough to go back to Greene County for the presidential election. Arriving in Cameron on November 2, 1864, he began walking the eight miles to his family's farm near Jacktown. Along the way, he met John Loughridge, "a staunch old democrat in a farm wagon," who gave him a ride. Loughridge peppered him with questions; but when the man asked Scherich if he was sorry he went in the army, Scherich told him, "Let me out of your old wagon, I will not ride with an old Copperhead."

While at home, Scherich, a few months short of twenty-one years old, went to the polls to vote:

> I was at home twenty days and voted for Lincoln to be president for a second term. Dr. Gray, who had been our family physician for years, challenged my vote, saying that I was not twenty-one years old. Steve Knight, president of the election board, as strong a democrat as the doctor and had been the undertaker for three funerals in our family, and knew my age as well as the doctor, asked me if I was twenty-one. My reply was that I was mustered into the service as twenty-one. Then he says will you swear to that? My reply was yes. Then he asked me to come inside, he wrote a statement to that effect I signed and swore to it. He took my ticket and as he put it in the box says you have earned the right to vote if you were only ten years old.[39]

The Congressional election that year also contained some interesting developments. Congressman Lazear was running for reelection in the 24th District, including Greene County. He was opposed by a Republican from Washington County, former Speaker of the state senate, George V. Lawrence. Lawrence, the son of former Pennsylvania state assemblyman and United States Congressman Joseph

Lawrence, had been born in Washington County on November 13, 1819. He came from a political family. In addition to his father, he also had two uncles who had been elected to the Pennsylvania Assembly from Beaver County in the 1820s. His own brother, William, had been elected to the state legislature to represent Dauphin County in 1858 and 1860. Another brother, Samuel, was sent to the state legislature by Warren County in 1860. Having received a liberal education, George V. Lawrence, devoted himself exclusively to agriculture and politics. Lawrence earned a reputation for tenacity in upholding the principles of the Republican Party. He was an experienced legislator, serving four terms in the Pennsylvania state house in 1843, 1847, 1858, and 1859. In addition, he was elected to the state Senate in 1848, 1849, 1850, 1851, and 1860. Lawrence was chosen Speaker of the state senate in 1861 and served in that capacity until 1863. Democratic newspapers referred to him as "the Abolition Speaker of the Senate." They also believed that Lawrence had been instrumental in trying to dilute the Democratic Party influence of Greene County voters on state politics by maneuvering it into the newly-created Twenty-fourth Congressional District, along with Washington, Beaver, and Lawrence counties on Pennsylvania's western border.[40] The Union Party of Greene County was the first to declare the nomination of Lawrence. At the county Union convention in May, Lawrence "received every vote but one." In addition, the Greene County conferees passed resolutions calling for continuation of the war, approving enfranchisement of soldiers in the field, and "avowing a fixed purpose to labor earnestly for the re-election of Abraham Lincoln."[41]

State Republican leaders seemed confident that the election would go their way. The *Franklin Repository* believed that in the fall, "Union strength at home cannot be short of the vote given for Gov. Curtin, unless we should have decisive disasters in the field . . . ."[42] Among several changes in Congress anticipated by the newspaper was that Congressman Lazear would be succeeded by George V. Lawrence. On September 27, 1864, Simon Cameron wrote to President Lincoln from Pittsburgh that all "is right in every district except the one" containing Westmoreland County, where Senator Edgar Cowan lived.[43] Two days later, Cameron gave a speech before a large Union meeting in Pittsburgh. Among the other speakers at the rally, which included ex-governor William F. Johnston and Congressman John Covode, was J. A. J. Buchanan of Greene County. The Pittsburgh papers described Buchanan as "an old Douglas Democrat."[44]

When Lawrence did indeed defeat Lazear in October, however, *The Waynesburg Messenger*, in an article published on October 12, 1864, howled that the "military was posted in several of the upper townships." Smelling a conspiracy by local Republican leaders, the editor noted that he had "the very best authority" for saying that Secretary of War Stanton issued an order directing that a regiment of soldiers be sent into Greene County to be present for the election. Noting that the order was given for the purpose of "INTIMIDATING THE DISAFFECTED," he was convinced the troops were present for the sole purpose of helping the Republicans defeat Lazear for Congress. Refusing to reveal its source, the *Messenger* reported ". . . we know one Lincoln office holder who exultantly expressed the belief to the other precious scamps . . . that this movement `would reduce the majority in Greene County for Gen. Lazear, to twelve hundred.'" Despite the fact that the county gave Lazear a majority of about 1600, the Democratic newspaper was certain that "judging from Richhill [Township], Lazear's majority may, by this foul means, be reduced below that of the Governor's election."[45]

The exact source of the *Messenger*'s information regarding such an order for troops to be present for the election in Greene County is difficult to trace. According to the *Official Records of the War of the Rebellion*, the commander of the Department of the Susquehanna, including western Pennsylvania, issued a special order on November 1, 1864. In these instructions to the district's provost marshals, it was directed that in "view of the approaching election, deserters from the army and the draft may return to their homes, and every effort must be made to arrest and hold them to the service they owe their Government."[46] It is possible that a similar order was issued prior to the state elections in October. Moreover, increasing publicity given assaults and violence between political factions in the county may have prompted a request by local Unionists for military protection at the polling places.

143

This was not necessarily an unusual move in areas north of the war zone that were prone to violent political unrest. General George McClellan, Democratic Presidential candidate in 1864, set the precedent by stationing soldiers at various polling places in Maryland during the 1861 fall elections.[47]

At any rate, the *Messenger* reported in mid-October, "The impression was quietly spread among certain timid men, that violence might arise at the polls, that certain persons would be arrested, and resistance would probably result &c." The arrest of deserters by men of Company F, 16th Regiment V. R. C., the search for draft resistors and draft dodgers, and the actions of "spying abolitionists" in the county who pointed out suspected deserters by spotting those with horses or other government property in their possession had an impact on the community. "[I]n many instances arrests were made and parties put to disgrace, expense and imprisonment, with scarcely a show of excuse." The editors noted that all "these things produced apprehension and alarm in the minds of timid people. The result shows," according to the Democratic newspaper, "that those who engineered these things, calculated well the effect." It was admitted, however, that in regard to the arrest of deserters in the county, "who, in many instances had taken bounties and shirked their duties, the only complaint that could be made was the *time* selected for their arrest."[48]

When the soldiers stationed in Waynesburg left for their barracks in New Brighton, Pennsylvania, on December 6, 1864, moreover, it was stated that the "best and kindest of feelings have [been] created between our citizens and these soldiers, since their sojourn among us." Officers with the veteran reserve corps "expressed surprise that instead of finding the nest of Rebellion . . . they found a peaceable, loyal, civil and quiet community."[49] Captain Randlett expressed thanks to the citizens of Waynesburg "for the many favors received from them." As he prepared to take his command out of the county, he stated that they were leaving "with regret, and the citizens of Waynesburg will be always kindly remembered by the members of Company 'F,' 16th Regiment, V. R. C."[50]

---

[1] *Greene County Republican* as quoted by the *Pennsylvania Daily Telegraph* (Harrisburg), 28 September 1864, p. 3.

[2] Letter from Edgar Cowan to Abraham Lincoln (Lincoln Papers at the Library of Congress), 17 June 1863.

[3] Letter from A. G. Curtin to Abraham Lincoln (Lincoln Papers at Library of Congress), 6 October 1864.

[4] *Franklin Repository* (Chambersburg, PA), 29 June 1864, p. 4. The article contains a table showing votes for governor in the 1863 general election for each of the counties comprising the 24th Congressional District of PA.

[5] *Waynesburg Messenger*, 2 April 1862, p. 2.

[6] *Ibid*, 18 June 1862, p. 3.

[7] *Ibid*, 6 August 1862, p. 3.

[8] *Ibid*, 7 April 1863, p. 3.

[9] *Ibid*, 25 March 1863, p. 3.

[10] *Ibid*, 1 April 1863, p. 2.

[11] *Ibid*, 7 April 1863, p. 3.

[12] *Ibid*, 22 April 1863, p. 3; 23 September 1863, p. 3.

[13] *Greene County Republican* as quoted by the *Waynesburg Messenger*, 6 May 1863, p. 3.

[14] *Waynesburg Messenger*, 6 May 1863, p. 3.

[15] *Ibid*.

[16] *Ibid*.

[17] *The Press* (Philadelphia), 26 May 1863, p. 2.

[18] *Waynesburg Messenger*, 17 June 1863, p. 3.

[19] *Ibid*, 7 October 1863, p. 3.

[20] *Greene County Republican* as quoted by the *Waynesburg Messenger*, 11 November 1863, p. 2.

[21] Letter from John C. Flenniken to John Lindsey (collection of Greene County Historical Society, Waynesburg, PA), 21 September 1863.

[22] *Lancaster Intelligencer*, 14 July 1863, p. 2.

[23] *Franklin Repository*, 11 November 1863, p. 4.

[24] *Daily Patriot and Union* (Harrisburg, PA), 17 July 1863, p. 2.

[25] *Evening Telegraph* (Harrisburg, PA), 25 September 1863, p. 2.

[26] "The 18th Pennsylvania Rides Again!!," a transcription of the journal of Private Isaac Scherich, Company A, 18th Pennsylvania Cavalry (available at the Cornerstone Genealogical Society, Waynesburg, PA), entry for 6 July 1863. The original of Isaac Scherich's journal is in the Trans-Appalachian Room of the Waynesburg University Library, Waynesburg, PA. Also see Boyd Crumrine, *The Courts of Justice, Bench and Bar of Washington County, Pennsylvania* (Chicago: R.R. Donnelley and Sons, 1902), p. 58.

[27] *The Press* (Philadelphia), 5 October 1863, p. 4.

[28] *Ibid.*

[29] *Waynesburg Messenger*, 7 October 1863, p. 3.

[30] *Franklin Repository*, 11 November 1863, p. 4.

[31] *Evening Telegraph* (Harrisburg), 28 October 1863, p. 3.

[32] *Waynesburg Messenger,* 16 March 1864, p. 2; 4 May 1864, p. 2.

[33] *Waynesburg Messenger,* 14 January 1863, p. 3.

[34] *Ibid,* 18 March 1863, p. 3.

[35] *Ibid,* 10 February 1864, p. 2.

[36] *Ibid,* 27 April 1864, p. 3.

[37] *Ibid,* 11 May 1864, p. 2.

[38] Journal of Isaac W. Scherich, p. 39.

[39] Journal of Isaac W. Scherich, p. 45.

[40] William Rodearmel, *Potraits of the Heads of State and Sketches of Members of the Legislature of Pennsylvania 1893-1894* (Harrisburg: E. K. Myers Printing Houses, 1893), p. 257; *Waynesburg Messenger*, 29 October 1862, p. 2.

[41] *Evening Telegraph*, 20 May 1864, p. 2.

[42] *Franklin Repository*, 29 June 1864, p. 4.

[43] Simon Cameron to Abraham Lincoln (Lincoln Papers at Library of Congress, Series I), 27 September 1864.

[44] *The Press* (Philadelphia), 1 October 1864, p. 1.

[45] *The Waynesburg Messenger*, 12 October 1864, p. 3.

[46] O.R., Series I, Vol. 43, pt. 2, p. 523.

[47] O.R., Series II, Vol. 1, p. 608; *The Press* (Philadelphia), 24 March 1864, p. 2.

[48] *Waynesburg Messenger,* 19 October 1864, p. 2.

[49] *Ibid,* 7 December 1864, p. 3.

[50] *Ibid,* 30 November 1864, p. 3.

Home Front Vignette: "The Death of Judge Lindsey!"

[John Lindsey and his family suffered a further loss in September 1864 with the unexpected death of his son, Judge James Lindsey. Judge Lindsey, as well as his younger brother, William Lindsey, was known as an outstanding leader of the Greene County Bench and Bar and the whole community. The Waynesburg Messenger reported the death of Judge Lindsey on September 7, 1864.]

"Our community was startled on Friday morning last, by the announcement that Judge Lindsey was dead! His demise took place at his residence, some six miles west of this place, about the middle of the previous night. It was known to but few that he had been unwell. He had held court at Washington the previous week, from which he returned, it seems, quite unwell, just a week previous to his death. He had what was regarded as a slight attack of Bilious Fever, before he went to Washington. After his return he rapidly became worse, but no one seemed to apprehend a fatal termination, till quite near the period of his death.

This sudden demise of Judge Lindsey has thrown a gloom over our entire community. He had a wide circle of relatives, and yet a much wider circle of attached and devoted friends. In the social circle, as a citizen, and Judge of the Court, his death creates a painful void. He had not yet reached the peak of life, nor the full vigor of manhood – being less than thirty-seven years of age – at the time of his death. Long years of matured usefulness seemed yet before him; but death, inexorable in his decrees, had otherwise willed!

How true, in regard to all of us, is the language of the poet:

A few months may – a few years must,
Repose us in the silent dust!

Judge Lindsey had been on the Bench about four years at the time of his decease. On account of his youth and apparent inexperience, he entered upon the discharge of his duties as Judge, with some distrust on the part of some of his brethren at the bar, as well as the community, to whom he was to administer the law, but he rapidly won the confidence of both and, it is believed that, at the time of his death, but few, if any, of our Judges, had to a greater extent, the confidence and respect both of Bar and people. This is not the language of eulogy and those who knew him and know the facts, will recognize the literal truth of the representation. He had a vigorous and well-balanced mind, rapid in its operations, and capable of mastering, apparently, without effort, the most intricate questions presented for solution, and a happy facility, both as an advocate and as a Judge, in conveying to a Jury the conclusions to which he had arrived."

Afterword

There is still research to be done before a complete picture of Greene County during the Civil War period can be drawn. The present work has done little more than create a sketch. The traditional county historians in the nineteenth century chose to ignore many of the episodes related here and to concentrate on the county's military contribution to the war. Events were probably too recent and internecine wounds in the county had not healed enough for dispassionate reflection. Greene County, like the country at large, was certainly divided. There were at least three factions of political and social opinions in the county. These included Republicans, who whole-heartedly supported the Lincoln administration in its political agenda and war policies, War Democrats, who were willing to align with Lincoln to see the war successfully concluded and the Union restored, and Peace Democrats, the majority in Greene, who stubbornly opposed many of Lincoln's war measures and called for compromise with the South. The strong support given Jesse Lazear in 1860, 1862, and 1864, by the voters of the county in the general elections those years seems to indicate a general satisfaction by the majority of Greene County citizens with his stand against the Lincoln administration. Once the war was over, however, the residents of the county concentrated their efforts in ventures like railroads, oil, gas, western cattle, and sheep. Bates, Evans, Hanna, and Waychoff decided not to dwell on the unpleasantness of the recent past.

For modern historians and genealogists interested in the problem, sources are difficult to find. Surviving editions of Greene County newspapers from the era are limited. Many letters and diaries of Greene County soldiers and civilians are still locked away in the county's attics. It is possible we may now never know more than a bare minimum of the story. After the war, many Peace Democrats simply destroyed their personal papers. Yet there are many untapped resources. It was common for local political leaders to report conditions to state and national party leaders. It may be that a search of relevant manuscript collections will shed more light. In addition, a thorough search needs to be made in the provost marshal records at the National Archives in Washington, D.C. Other resources may eventually come to be recognized. Whatever future research discloses, it is important that more work is done.

After the war, it appears that the citizens of Greene County did the best they could to forget. Before the war, in 1853, county leaders had started a movement to construct a railroad connecting Waynesburg to the Monongahela Valley. On January 5, 1853, a meeting was held at the Hamilton House in Waynesburg to discuss a railroad project to the Hempfield Road. Citizens from Waynesburg and the vicinity passed a resolution approving and recommending construction of a line from Waynesburg to Monongahela City, by way of Beallsville.[1] As developments continued in the Dunkard oil field, in February 1865, promoters sought to incorporate a railroad that would cross the county from the mouth of Dunkard Creek to the western boundary. With a capital stock of half a million dollars, it was hoped that the line would "bring into communication with the civilized world, those dwellers near the boundary line of West Virginia, who now depend upon their nags for transportation." A bill incorporating the Greene County Railroad Company was passed by the state senate on February 25, 1865. Another scheme was for a railroad from Waynesburg via the South Branch of Ten Mile Creek and the Monongahela River to Brownsville. Promoters for the Waynesburg and Monongahela River Railroad Company met at Waynesburg on February 11, 1865. None of these railroad projects came to fruition, but railroad fever swept the county as the Civil War drew to a close.[2]

The *Waynesburg Messenger* avidly supported all these hopes for a county railroad. "The valley of Ten Mile is the natural route of communications between Waynesburg and the Monongahela river," the paper commented, "and indeed between the latter point and the Ohio river." The route had been previously surveyed by the B&O Railroad, who had decided it was the shortest line between the two rivers. Politics at that time, however, had kept Greene County from benefitting from the survey. Now, the "farming interests, our coal lands, and our Oil prospects all call for this improvement," the *Messenger* concluded, "let us have it."[3] By the fall of 1864, agricultural land in Ten Mile Valley was advancing in value. Completion of the proposed railroad was expected to only make the future brighter. Already, in the eastern end of the valley, "purchasers" of farm land were "becoming more plenty than sellers, especially in the neighborhood of Jefferson and Clarksville."[4] Former county enrollment officer, W. G. W. Day, joined in the railroad mania. After purchasing the *Waynesburg Republican,* he became a promoter of the Waynesburg and Washington Railroad, which started operation in 1877.

As veterans returned home after the end of the war, a movement began to organize a soldier's union in Greene County. Veterans and representatives of deceased soldiers met at the Court House in Waynesburg on August 12, 1865. Joseph Cooke was appointed president with G. Dougherty and Harper Rex as vice presidents. A. V. Dillie and E. Y. Johns served as secretaries for the meeting. It was noted that the main object of the soldiers union was "to regulate and obtain employment for honorably discharged soldiers." The meeting passed several resolutions calling for a united effort to care for those soldiers unable to work and bury those that died. The group also pledged to "place a protecting arm about the widows and orphans of deceased soldiers, and prevent them becoming in the slightest manner objects of charity." They also agreed to petition Congress to pay the same bounty to soldiers who enlisted in 1861 and 1862, or to their widows and orphans, as bounties paid recruits after 1862. A committee was appointed to obtain signatures for such a petition for presentation to Congress. Members of the committee from each township included: Aleppo – Azariah Evans, Centre – James H. Fordyce, Richhill – A. V. Dillie, Franklin – E. Y. Johns, Jefferson – John Rex, Marion – James Woods, Esq., Cumberland – Franklin Gwinn, Whitely – J. G. Fordyce, Wayne – Thomas Longstreth, Jackson – Thomas Weaver, Washington – Newton Keigley, Morgan – Jackson Young, Perry – E. J. Rose, Morris – G. W. Nicely, Springhill – Maxwell Plantz, Greene – Jesse Fordyce, Dunkard – George W. Boyers, and Monongahela – George F. Stone. The meeting was addressed by Reverend James Sloan, President of Waynesburg High School, and Reverend J. Laughlin, a veteran of the 7th (West) Virginia Infantry. It was noted that "large numbers" participated in the meeting.[5] This 1865 gathering was a precursor to the eventual organization on September 7, 1883 of the J. F. McCullough Post, No. 367, Grand Army of the Republic.[6] In 1898 and 1899, the county remembered its veterans with a finely constructed monument erected in the East Park of Waynesburg, now called Monument Park, that at one time had been part of the Commons.

In Perry Township, Reuben Brown, no doubt still mourning the senseless death of his son, William, continued farming. L. K. Evans, before taking off for the Midwest, busied himself researching and writing his pioneer histories of the county. In January, before leaving Congress in 1865, Jesse Lazear drafted a letter advising his constituents of his view of Lincoln's reconstruction plans after the conclusion of the war:

> I believe we are going to have peace on the basis of a restored Union. I think, I am posted on this subject. Mr. Lincoln, in my opinion, will accept a return of the South, without requiring general emancipation, but the slavery question to remain as it is under the constitution. A full and free amnesty to all, and a fair and liberal adjustment of other questions growing out of the Rebellion. I may be mistaken, but I believe I am correct in my views and hopes.[7]

After serving for a time as chairman of the Democratic Party in Greene County, Lazear retired, in 1867, to "Windsor Mill Farm," his Baltimore County, Maryland, country home, his remains being returned to Greene County to be buried in Green Mount Cemetery in 1877. In the meantime, Republicans, George V. Lawrence and, later, J. B. Donley, represented Greene County in Congress from 1865 until 1871. Donley, a native of Mount Morris, became a professor at Abingdon College, Abingdon, Illinois, after graduating from Waynesburg College in 1859. In 1862, he became Captain of Company I, 83rd Illinois Infantry. After the war, he attended law school in Albany, New York, and then practiced law in Waynesburg until he was elected to Congress in 1868.[8]

Dr. Alexander Patton returned from Harrisburg after serving two terms in the legislature, later being elected to serve in the state Senate. His successor in the Pennsylvania House, Democrat, Dr. Thomas Rose, elected in October 1864, continued Dr. Patton's opposition to Republican policies as the war drew to a close in 1865. Rose voted against ratification of the Thirteenth Amendment to the United States Constitution, the amendment abolishing slavery. In a speech before the Pennsylvania Assembly, Rose objected to the way that supporters of ratification were disposed "to bully down, to annoy, to deter us [the opposition] from expressing our sentiments upon this grave question." Although Rose believed that Pennsylvania had rightly decided years before to abolish slavery within the commonwealth, he doubted the validity of the state or Congress acting against the institution in other states. Denying Congress' power to propose such an amendment, he emphasized his unwillingness to tamper with the Constitution, "either directly, or indirectly." He succinctly stated his position:

> I do not uphold slavery. I detest the rebellion. I am willing to let slavery die. Some gentlemen have said that we are not willing to let slavery die. I am willing to let it die. I want nothing at all to do with it but my intention is to vote against this resolution.[9]

District Provost Marshal, Captain John Cuthbertson, eventually succumbed to his war wounds and died on September 20, 1865, after a short illness at his home in New Brighton, Pennsylvania. The Chambersburg *Franklin Repository* observed that Cuthbertson "performed his duty as a soldier in a creditable manner, and only left his regiment when disabled by wounds." As provost marshal of the Twenty-Fourth District of Pennsylvania, the Chambersburg paper noted he had "rendered entire satisfaction, both to the Government and the citizens of the district." His death was mourned by "hosts of warm friends," who remembered him as "an upright citizen, a brave soldier, and an honest man."[10]

As the war concluded, Greene County continued to experience its first oil boom along Dunkard Creek. The Dunkard oil eventually dried up, but the county soon found itself in a second oil boom in the 1880s, also fueled by drilling for natural gas. Davistown, as the oil and gas booms subsided in Dunkard Township, became a picturesque little village nestled in the hills on a backcountry road, little remembering the visits made there by federal troops during the war years. In Morris Township, James Fonner's daughter married, and the old sheep shed, the scene of her hopes and fears, fell into decay, rotting away, leaving nothing but the ghost of a family legend.

---

[1] *Daily Morning Post* (Pittsburgh), 15 January 1853, p. 2.

[2] *Daily Evening Bulletin* (Philadelphia), 3 February 1865, p. 5; *The Press* (Philadelphia), 25 February 1865, p. 2; *Waynesburg Messenger,* 8 February 1865, p. 3.

[3] *Waynesburg Messenger,* 19 October 1864, p. 3.

[4] *Ibid*

[5] *Waynesburg Messenger*, 16 August 1865, p. 2.

[6] J. F. McCullough Post 367 of the G. A. R., "Memorial Day 1908 Waynesburg, PA, Souvenir Program"

[7] *Ibid,* 1 February 1865, p. 2.

[8] Bates, pp. 658-659.

[9] *Waynesburg Messenger,* 1 March 1865, p. 3.

[10] *Franklin Repository* (Chambersburg, PA), 11 October 1865, p. 2.

APPENDIX A: ". . . erection of the house for the employment of the Poor."

During the Jacksonian Era of American history, the country decided that social problems such as crime, poverty, and mental illness could best be handled by isolating those who suffered with these conditions from the corrupting influence of their environment. Penitentiaries were constructed on either the Pennsylvania system or the New York system to provide a public institution where criminals could be taught religious values and a useful trade to make them productive citizens when they were eventually released. Insane asylums were constructed for confining the mentally ill; and poor houses or poor farms were financed by state and local governments as a means of caring for extreme cases of poverty by providing the poor with shelter and some form of meaningful employment until they could regain their proper place in society. Greene County was no exception, and in 1861, under authority of state law, the county commissioners decided to purchase a farm that could be renovated to allow the county to care for its own paupers and mentally ill in a modern institutional setting.

Accordingly, Barnet Whitlatch, Jacob Loar, and William Davis were appointed acting commissioners for the erection of a house for employment of the Poor. The county purchased a farm from R. W. Downey, located in Franklin Township, on the site now occupied by the Greene County Historical Society Museum, for a price of $5,000.00. Contractors Sayers and Grove were paid $7,000.00 for constructing the house and an additional $1,544.26 was paid by the commissioners for building a porch, stable, smokehouse, and privies. For their services, Loar and Davis were paid fees of $97.50 and $94.50 respectively. Whitlatch received slightly over $120.00 as a commissioner fee and to superintend the farm.[1] The Poor House Directors, Charles A. Black, Aaron Shelby, and William Davis, published an auditor's report, February 4, 1863, detailing the institution's account with the county to January 1, 1863. The facilities operating budget was $3,404.65. The report noted

---

[1] *Waynesburg Messenger,* 3 February 1864, p. 3.

"that a large portion of the expenditures so far made were for stock and the necessary implements for the farm, and furniture for the house." It was also stated that the "house was unfinished, at least so far as the safety and comfort of the insane paupers were concerned; and considerable expense had to be incurred in arranging a room for the most violent of them." This appears to have been the first year of occupation of the facility as additional expenses pointed out by the directors included fences, planting an orchard, and bedding for the residents. In 1862, the farm housed as many as forty-nine paupers, with eleven, the largest number, coming from Wayne Township. Eight residents were listed as "insane and deranged," two of them considered violent and needing confinement. The farm boasted two horses, a yoke of oxen, four cows, two sows and seven pigs.[2]

For the year ending January 1, 1864, the Poor House Directors, with Daniel Fuller replacing C. A. Black, reported operating costs of $4,261.79. The farm steward was paid a salary of $355.15, slightly less than a dollar per day. The farm was occupied by as high as eighty-two paupers, seven being considered "insane and partially deranged." The lack of adequate space for these insane paupers was a concern for the directors:

> We also again refer to the utter unfitness of the building under its present arrangement for the proper and humane care of insane paupers. One room has been fitted up, so that some degree of comfort and security has been attained; but if the insane of the County now at Harrisburg and Pittsburg hospitals, are brought home, and put in our house of employment, as is now the intention to do, some suitable provision must at once be made for their reception. This will necessarily involve us in considerable expense, which might have been avoided by a different arrangement of the rooms when the house was built. It was not however, we presume, contemplated at the time, that the insane paupers should occupy the same building and hence no suitable

---

[2] *Ibid,* 4 February 1863, p. 3.

provision was made for such.[3]

When the Grand Jury for the December Session of Court inspected the property on December 23, 1863, the jurors agreed that "the rooms allotted to the insane paupers are not well calculated to insure the comfort and safety of the unfortunate inmates." It was reported, however, that "under the arrangement of the House, no other or better plan could be adopted." Overall, the jurors found the facility to be "in a most creditable condition—as much as they think possible under the disadvantages under which the steward and matron have labored." The residents were well cared for and no cause for complaint was found. To the contrary, they believed the steward had "most faithfully discharged his duty," and the matron was "admirably qualified for the position she occupies." They reported that her "industry, care and attention in providing for the comfort of the unfortunate inmates" called for "the approbation of every person interested in the institution."[4]

By 1864, business at the Poor Farm grew briskly. Costs exceeded $6,000.00. A barn was built for $406.00, much of the lumber being obtained on the farm itself and cut on a portable steam saw. One hundred thirteen inmates had been received into the facility. The greatest number present at any time during the year had been about seventy-five. Insane and partly deranged residents numbered ten. Although the Steward, Elijah Adams, reported making one hundred and fifty-nine gallons of molasses from a little more than an acre of cane, the farm produce did not yet meet the needs of the residents, and the directors noted that everything else needed for consumption by the inmates had "to be bought at present enormous prices." The board, which now also consisted of Arthur Rinehart, believed that even with the higher prices, the actual cost of caring for the county's paupers was "far less than under the old system."[5]

---

[3] *Waynesburg Messenger*, 3 February 1864, p. 3.

[4] *Ibid*, 20 January 1864, p. 3.

[5] *Waynesburg Messenger, 9 November 1864, p. 3;* 8 February 1865, p. 3.

APPENDIX B: Captain William C. Lindsey, Company A, 18th Pennsylvania Cavalry

Judge Lindsey and his younger brother, William C. Lindsey, were two Greene County lawyers who no doubt would have had much to offer as future leaders of the county after the war. Tragically, for both the Lindsey family and the community, both men died before the conflict ran its course. Judge Lindsey died from bilious fever in the early fall of 1864, and his brother, Captain Lindsey, died in action at Hagerstown, Maryland, shortly after the Battle of Gettysburg, on July 6, 1863. The Waynesburg and Jefferson communities were certainly shocked to learn of Captain Lindsey's death. "No death has occurred among the gallant sons of Little Greene, since the war began," reported the *Messenger,* "which has been more generally and profoundly regretted than that of Captain Lindsey."[6] When his body was interred at Jefferson, Pennsylvania, after being escorted home from Hagerstown by his brother, Judge Lindsey, the Free Masons, the Odd Fellows, members of the Greene County Bar, and "a great concourse of citizens" participated in the funeral procession. The Waynesburg newspapers expressed the grief of the mourners, noting that he "was, indeed, loved by all who knew him; and in his early death the community has suffered a loss which cannot be easily repaired."[7]

At the commencement of the war, William Lindsey was serving as a clerk in the United States Patent Office in Washington, D.C. Shortly after Lincoln's call for troops to put down the rebellion, Lindsey enlisted as a private in a company of Washington, D.C., militia. After the expiration of his term of enlistment, Lindsey returned to work in the Patent Office. He soon, however, became a victim of party patronage. Despite his early show of patriotism and the efficiency with which he discharged his official duties, his membership in the Democratic Party was a liability. In the fall of 1861, Lindsey was given a "furlough" from his duties at the Patent Office. It was reported

---

[6] *Waynesburg Messenger,* 22 July 1863, p. 3
[7] *Ibid,* 29 July 1863, p. 3.

that the furlough was "likely to last till the incoming of a Democratic Administration." The *Waynesburg Messenger* saw the action as a fine example of "the spirit and practice of the men who talk so glibly and persistently of giving up 'party' for 'country.'" "No charge of incompetency or neglect of duty was brought against him," the paper remarked, "his Democratic principles and affiliations constituted the 'head and front of his offending;' and for these he received peremptory 'leave to quit.'"[8]

Upon his return to Greene County, William Lindsey completed his legal studies and was admitted to practice law in the several county courts. Shortly after his admission to the Bar, J. A. J. Buchanan announced that Lindsey would be joining him in his practice. Buchanan had been partners with James Lindsey before the older brother was elected to the Bench. Buchanan was known "as one of the ripest lawyers and ablest advocates at" the county Bar, "and has met with large and flattering professional success." It was expected that the Judge's brother, who was "a young gentleman of fine talents and courteous bearing," would "make a popular Attorney."[9] After his death, the members of the local Bar passed a resolution that Lindsey had indeed been, in his short career, "an able though honorable practitioner; a severe critic of the literature as well as learning of the Bar, and a high-toned and courteous gentleman."[10]

Lindsey was elected Captain of the Greene County volunteers who became Company A, 18th Pennsylvania Cavalry, in the fall of 1862. Isaac Sherich has a couple of interesting stories about Lindsey in his memoir. On one April morning in 1863 about four A.M., Scherich relates that he was awakened by the crowing of an old rooster a few feet from where he lay. He soon put a stop to the rooster's crow, and a further investigation revealed a pig in a little pen nearby. It was not long before the rooster and pig had been distributed among the members of Company A for breakfast. A nice piece of pork was given to Bill Johnson, a black man who served as cook for the officers. Not long after breakfast, Captain Lindsey came

[8] *Waynesburg Messenger,* 23 October 1861, p. 3.
[9] *Ibid,* 25 December 1861, p. 3; 1 January 1862, p. 3.
[10] *Ibid,* 12 August 1863, p. 2.

around with a complaint from the brigade commander that someone had taken a chicken and a pig from a nearby house, and he asked the men if they knew anything about the matter. Someone said, "Captain, did you not have pork for breakfast?" Sherich wrote that Lindsey just turned and walked away. That was the last they ever heard about the matter.

After the Battle of Gettysburg, on the night of July 3, Sherich described a thunderstorm that saturated the ground, making it difficult to find a dry spot to sleep. He found a rail fence and fashioned a rough bed by taking two rails and propping one end about two feet from the ground on the fence and allowing the other end to remain on the ground. He had just settled down to sleep when Captain Lindsey stumbled over him in the dark. The Captain told him he was "nearly dead for want of sleep," and he was wandering around searching for a dry spot. Lindsey was impressed with Sherich's rail bed, so Sherich helped him fashion his own bed. While most of the company slept on the wet ground, Captain Lindsey told him he had experienced "a fine nights[sic] sleep."

A few days later, near Boonesboro, Maryland, on the morning of July 6, 1863, Sherich went to see Lindsey to obtain a pass so he could go into the town to find a hat, his cap having fallen off during the night march to Boonesboro. Lindsey told him that he would not need a pass if he went with him into town, and so a short while later the two of them rode into Boonesboro. Sherich got a hat and then sat on his horse holding the reins of Lindsey's horse while the Captain spent some time in a nearby saloon with some other officers. While waiting, Scherich watched their division ride through town with the 18th Pennsylvania in the lead. When Lindsey came out, they rode along the side of the column and through some fields, finally catching up to the regiment after a hard ride. Scherich was then assigned to Sergeant Will Smith and three other troopers as an advance guard. Near Hagerstown, Maryland, after the advance exchanged shots with a rebel vidette, Sherich and Nick Kent were posted on a road turning to the right toward Antietam Creek. From their position on a bluff about five hundred yards down the road, Sherich could see up the main street of Hagerstown, almost to the town square, where a formation of J. E. B. Stuart's cavalry was stationed as a rear guard for the

Army of Northern Virginia. He watched as the first battalion of the 18th Pennsylvania, including Captain Lindsey and Company A, charged into the town. He observed the enemy force being driven back to the square where a melee occurred, some of the men using sabers and some using revolvers.[11]

Just a few short weeks before the engagements at Gettysburg and Hagerstown, William Lindsey had been home on sick leave. A fever had kept him home for several weeks, but when word was received of Lee's invasion into Pennsylvania, he refused to continue his leave of absence and determined to join his command. Now, at the head of the 18th Pennsylvania Cavalry's First Battalion, he charged at a gallop down the National Road into Hagerstown. As they entered the town, the color bearer, Thomas Eagon, was killed. As they neared the square, Lindsey unhorsed one Confederate with a saber blow. Then engaged with three more, he was shot in the left side of the throat. With Lindsey still in the saddle, his horse turned down South Potomac Street, where he was again shot, this time through the body. At that point he fell dead from his horse. Lieutenant B. F. Campbell, at almost the same moment, had his horse killed under him and was rendered unconscious by the fall. When he recovered, he discovered Lindsey's body nearby, and he assisted Dr. Henry Capeheart to carry the Captain to a nearby house where the family promised to bury him and mark the grave. The town was occupied by both Union and Confederate cavalry throughout the day, but finally, numbers forced the Union troopers to retire down the road toward Williamsport.[12]

Word of his death reached Lindsey's family through the editors of the *Messenger*. "We have never been charged with a more painful task than that of imparting the tidings of this unhappy event to the family of the deceased," Jennings and Jones reported, "and we trust we shall never again be compelled to witness such a scene of heart-breaking anguish as followed the announcement of their loss." The newspaper had received the news in a letter written from Philadelphia by J. A. J. Buchanan and George L. Wyly to Thomas C. Lazear in

---

[11] Journal of Isaac Scherich, pp. 10, 15-16.

[12] *Waynesburg Messenger*, 22 July 1863, p. 3; 29 July 1863, p. 3. Also see *O.R., Series I, Vol. 27, Part I, pp. 1005-1007, 1011.*

Pittsburgh. Buchanan and Wyly had seen a notice of Captain Lindsey's death in a Baltimore paper, and they went at once to Baltimore to ascertain more details about the event.[13] A few months later, Judge Lindsey received the following letter from the headquarters of the First Brigade of the Third Cavalry Division:

Comsy Dept
First Brig 3rd Div Cavalry Corps.
Culpepper, Va Oct 5th, 63

To the Honorable Judge Lindsey
Waynesburg Greene Co Pa
Judge
I have the honor to refer to you for instructions in regard to the disposition of Capt. Wm Lindsey's effects which are now in my possession The way I came in possession of them I will briefly state Capt. Frank Campbell after William's death carefully collected them put them in a box but having no means of sending them to Washington was necessitated to put them in his company wagon which was then in the brigade train After the train moved out it was found to be pretty heavily laden and through the influence of our quartermaster the Inspector Gen of this div came and ordered things to be thrown out and among them was the captains I discovered them and have been transporting them since that time in my headquarters wagon where they are perfectly safe until I see Capt Campbell who is at the front some 20 miles from here will consider myself responsible for the proper care of them as I know Frank was particularly careful of them and would not lose them for any consideration and as Will and I were intimate friends I feel obligated to see that you get them For many times we prize things that are not intrinsically valuable only so far as they associate with the memory of the departed
Capt. Will died while leading heroically his

[13] *Waynesburg Messenger,* 15 July 1863, p. 3.

company on to victory a noble honorable death

      hoping to hear from you at your earliest convenience

      I remain very respectful your obedient servant J S Beazell

      Lieutenant and A. C. S. 1st Brig 3rd Cavl Div[14]

In reviewing the results of the tragedy for the Lindsey family, Jennings and Jones of the *Messenger* wrote that Captain Lindsey "was a young man of fine promise, courteous, generous and honorable, and will be sincerely lamented by all who knew him."[15]

---

[14] Lt. J. S. Beazell to Honorable Judge Lindsey, 5 October 1863 (photocopy of letter in private collection of D. Kent Fonner, Beach Lake, PA. Original letter in archives of Greene County Historical Society Museum, Waynesburg, PA.)
[15] *Waynesburg Messenger,* 15 July 1863, p. 3.

APPENDIX C: Ordinance No. 1 of the Borough of Waynesburg

During the Civil War era, Waynesburg began to become more conscious of its station as the county seat, and municipal pride expressed itself in various institutions and new policies. In the 1850s, the town witnessed the erection of a new county courthouse, built from brick in a classic Greek revival style, complete with a portico of white, wooden Corinthian columns. The building was topped by a cupola, eventually supporting a statue of General Nathaniel Greene, carved from a poplar log. A second brick building topped by a cupola was built on the north side of the Commons at the top of Washington Street to house the newly established Waynesburg College. By the winter of 1865, the Waynesburg newspapers felt the necessity of calling the attention of the Waynesburg Borough Council to the "sad condition of our streets." As the winter continued, it was noted that "numerous heaps and ridges of ashes are allowed to remain, and are every day growing more beautifully large and numerous." Piling ashes and debris on the streets was now considered "a filthy practice and a burning shame, and, we fear, an everlasting disgrace." The creation of a town park on the Commons had met with full approval from the editors, and now civic pride demanded that "our 'city fathers' attend" to the removal of the piles of ashes on the streets "and put an embargo on any further transgressions."[16]

What the newspapers failed to note, however, was that on July 7, 1862, the "city fathers" had already taken steps to outlaw the activity complained of by enacting the Borough of Waynesburg's Ordinance No. 1. At that time, the Borough Council gave full enforcement powers to the Borough Constable, who was elected at each regular municipal election and who was entitled to receive the same fees as any township constable for similar services. Among the activities prohibited by the ordinance was the obstruction of the streets, allies, and sidewalks or borough pavements "by permitting timber, stone,

---

[16] *Waynesburg Messenger,* 8 February 1865, p. 3.

ashes, coal, wood, boxes, barrels, merchandize, or any other articles, or material calculated to obstruct, to remain upon . . . the street . . . for a period of more than twenty-four hours." Violators were subject to a fine of fifty cents for the first offense and one dollar for each subsequent violation. More specifically, the new ordinance provided a fine of no more than five dollars for any person "depositing ashes, shavings, or any other annoyance upon any footway or street." In addition, the ordinance placed a duty on all property owners to keep clean the portion of the streets and public ways adjacent to their property and to remove "all manner of filth or rubbish whatever." If such was not done for any five day period, then the Street Commissioner was authorized to clean that portion of the public way at the expense of the adjacent property owner and to add twenty percent on the cost as compensation for the Street Commissioner.

Other sections of the ordinance, besides maintaining order on the streets by providing laws against public drunkenness, fighting, and disturbing the peace, also sought to improve conditions in the town by regulating public sanitation and the grading, paving, and curbing of sidewalks. One section provided a fine of three dollars for every five day period that any person "owning a privy without a sufficient vault, or hog pen or stable upon or adjacent to any of the streets or allies of the borough, and permitting the filth to accumulate so as to be obnoxious to other residents." The depositing of dead animals or other noxious substances within borough limits was prohibited. Owners of lots on Main Street were required to "grade, curb, and pave" the sidewalks a distance of ten feet in front of each of their lots. Eliminating boardwalks and mud foot paths, the municipality required all foot ways on streets to be brick or stone. The sidewalks on Main Street were required to be ten feet wide from the front of the lots to the curb stone with a descent of nine inches to the curb stone. Of course, any riding, driving, leading, or hitching horses on any of the sidewalks was subject to a fine.

Keeping with the concern for civic improvement and the creation of a park on the north side of town, all persons were prohibited from using the Commons for a brickyard or a stone quarry, and no more stone was to be removed from any quarry already opened on the Commons. Slaughter houses were prohibited anywhere within the borough's jurisdictional limits. Licenses were required to be obtained from the Burgess for any circus show, menagerie, cake stands, or "itinerating beer, cider, cake or confectionery wagons" operating within the town.

Regulations of horses and hogs in the borough limits suggest the growth of Waynesburg from a rural village to a more urban setting. Any one "letting Stallions" within the borough limits was subject to a fine. Even exhibiting a stallion on the streets subjected the offender to a fine of three dollars for the first offense and five dollars for each subsequent violation. Training mares and geldings, either in harness or under saddle, through the streets and alleys was a violation of the law. Hogs in town were an apparently special nuisance, and the new ordinance provided that after October 1, 1862, all owners of hogs were to keep their animals confined to their own property or pens. Any hogs "found running at large, within the limits of said borough, after that date, shall be seized and sold by the Borough Constable, and the proceeds thereof be paid into the treasury."[17]

---

[17] *Waynesburg Messenger,* 30 July 1862, p. 2.

APPENDIX D: A Gallant and Patriotic Family

The *Waynesburg Messenger,* shortly after the Battle of Gettysburg, on July 22, 1863, described the patriotic efforts of one Greene County family in service to the Union. The example of these men was repeated by hundreds of others from the county:

> The Purmans of this county, are as gallant a band of brothers as ever drew sword in a just and patriotic cause. Already three of them have been badly wounded, indeed permanently disabled, in the war for the Union.
>
> Lieut. D. Gray Purman, of the 16th Wisconsin Volunteers, our readers will remember, was seriously wounded by both ball and shell, at the battle of Shiloh, while gallantly cheering on his men to the charge; indeed his clothes were literally riddled by bullets. He is not yet recovered from his wounds, and most likely never will.
>
> Next, Sgt. Nelson N. Purman was wounded at the battle of Chancellorsville, a rifle ball entering a shoulder and imbedding itself so deeply in the chest that it has neither been discovered nor removed, and in all probability never will be. He is slowly recovering, however, but will hardly be able to take the field again.
>
> And last, Lieut. J. Jackson Purman, of the 140th Regiment, Pennsylvania Volunteers, has been struck down, wounded in both legs at the battle of Gettysburg, and in one so badly that it had to be amputated.
>
> It is to such lads as these the Union cause owes its glorious triumphs, and we trust the country will cherish them, and all her brave defenders.
>
> A. A. Purman, Esq., of this place, is now in the East, and will return with his brother as soon as he can be removed.
>
> The Purmans are not men whose patriotism

evaporates in talk, and who stand on street corners and point out and mutter curses at "Copperheads." They seal their love of their country and government with their blood.

APPENDIX E: 168TH Regiment, Pennsylvania Militia

M. Lafayette Gordon, 85th Pennsylvania Infantry, wrote a letter to the *Waynesburg Messenger* on January 6, 1863, describing the unit's experiences in an expedition into North Carolina. From a camp near New Berne, North Carolina, Gordon reported that the "Greene County drafted men are here."[18] Gordon was referring to the men from Greene County conscripted in the Pennsylvania state draft in October 1862. The men had been mustered into service on October 16, 1862, and reported to Camp Howe near Pittsburgh in the latter part of October 1862. At Camp Howe, the Greene County draftees were organized with additional men drafted from Westmoreland, Fayette, Beaver, Allegheny, and Erie Counties into the 168th Regiment, Pennsylvania Militia. The regiment was to serve for nine months, and the Greene County men were assigned to Company A, commanded by Captain Hiram H. Cree. The men were issued their clothing and equipment on December 2, and that day the 168th Regiment, P. M., was sent to the front at Fortress Monroe in Virginia.[19] A correspondent from Company A, identified only as "A Live Lincoln Man," described the journey for the readers of the *Waynesburg Messenger:*

> We left Camp Howe about the 1st of December, under orders to report to Washington City, we left the busy "city of smoke" [Pittsburgh] on the evening train, and via Harrisburgh[sic] and Baltimore, arrived at our destination. Nothing of importance transpired *en route* except that we were very hospitably entertained by the Soldiers' Relief Association in Baltimore. The edibles were good, abundant, and served up in excellent style.[20]

The "Live Lincoln Man" noticed that the Whites in Baltimore

---

[18] *Waynesburg Messenger,* 25 February 1863, p. 2.
[19] Bates, *History of Pennsylvania Volunteers,* Vol. IV, p. 1134.
[20] *Waynesburg Messenger,* 15 April 1863, p. 2.

seemed "demure and silent," but occasionally, as they were leaving for Washington, D. C., "a slight degree of comfort to the 'drift'[sic]" came from a Black resident who would flash a "broad grin" and "sing out 'God bess de Yanky,' and give demonstrations of joy peculiar to their race." The men spent thirty-six hours in Washington, getting in a little sight-seeing before heading off on a transport ship, the "South America," down the Potomac River and the Chesapeake Bay to Fortress Monroe on the tip of the Virginia Peninsula.[21]

From Fortress Monroe, the regiment was ordered to Newport News, where it spent two weeks in additional training before being directed to Suffolk, Virginia, where the 168th Regiment, P. M., became part of Spinola's "Keystone Brigade." At Suffolk, it was noted that the "health of the Regiment" was "good." Families back home in Greene County were also advised that Captain Cree was "very popular with his men, being always with them and doing everything in his power for their comfort." "A Live Lincoln Man" described the men's time at Suffolk:

> We arrived late in the evening and went to the woods and made our fires; the night was cold and cheerless, and we learned to soldier in the true meaning of the term. By 4 o'clock the next day we had a beautiful camp; the heavy timber and thick copse gave way before the axe wielded by the stalwart arms of Pennsylvanians, and an air of comfort was felt and enjoyed. We have spent much of our time in moving from place to place. We had no sooner made ourselves comfortable when we were ordered to Newbern, N. C.[22]

The trip to New Berne included a sixty-mile march and river transport by way of the Chowan River.

The Keystone Brigade arrived at New Berne on January 1, 1863. Here the Greene County men, along with the rest of the regiment, were thoroughly drilled. They participated in several marches into the surrounding countryside, but never

---

[21] *Ibid.*
[22] *Waynesburg Messenger,* 15 April 1863, p. 2.

participated in any battle. After a while, the Keystone Brigade was sent to relieve the garrison at Little Washington, N. C. The 168th Regiment stayed here until the brigade was ordered to Fortress Monroe on June 28, 1863. From Fortress Monroe, the unit moved to White House, Virginia, to participate in a demonstration against Richmond led by General Dix. Upon receiving news of Robert E. Lee's invasion of Pennsylvania, the regiments of the Keystone Brigade expressed a desire to be led to the support of the Union army in Pennsylvania. They even expressed a willingness to serve beyond nine months if it became necessary. The brigade's request was granted; and the Keystone Brigade was directed to Harper's Ferry, where it occupied Maryland Heights. The Battle of Gettysburg having in the meantime already been fought, the regiment joined the Army of the Potomac at Boonesboro, Maryland. After Lee's army escaped across the Potomac, the 168th Regiment, P. M., was directed to Middletown, Maryland, and a few days later to Harrisburg. On July 25, 1863, the regiment was then mustered out of service; and, by August 5, the *Messenger* reported that Captain Cree and his men had returned to their homes in Greene County.[23] It should be noted that of the seventy-three drafted men who left the county in October 1862, three died. These included Sergeant James E. Burwell, who died at Washington, N. C., on June 22, 1863; John Kenner, who died at Washington, N. C., on June 29, 1863; and Joseph Minor, who died at Hampton, Va., on June 2, 1863.

[23] *Ibid,* 5 August 1863, p. 3.

Roster of Company A, 168TH Regiment, Pennsylvania Militia

Composed of men drafted from Greene County by the state military conscription in the Fall of 1862 [Source – Bates, *History of Pennsylvania Volunteers,* Vol. IV, pp. 1135-1136.]:

Hiram H. Cree, Captain
William F. Hughes, 1st Lieutentant
Jonathon M. Morris, 2nd Lieutenant

James Hudson, 1st Sergeant
Samuel Arnet, Sergeant
Thomas Craig, Sergeant
John Wundel, Sergeant
Archibald Grooms, Sergeant
James E. Burwell, Sergeant

Levi S. Patterson, Corporal
Robert C. Bennett, Corporal
William Dunn, Corporal
Lot S. Reib, Corporal
Joseph Moore, Corporal
Christian Ruse, Corporal
John W. Wilson, Corporal
William F. Smith, Corporal

Privates – John Anderson
John Ansley
Samuel Atkinson
William Barnhart
William Bowan
Joseph M. Bearmore
William E. Bennett
John Barnhart
William Booth
Charles Calvert

Alfred Cozzard
William Cluttler
Francis Clark
John H. Cummings
Morris Clark
Jacob Cumbridge
David C. Davidson
Benjamin Dean
Joseph Davidson
Lewis Demathers

Jeremiah Estle
Mathias Estle
John H. Evans
William Gass
Abram Gooseman
Hamilton Groom
Elizor Garrison
Ellis R. Garrison
Archibald Gribble
Harvey Hendershot
Griffith Herod
Joseph Headley
J. Thomas Huffman
Samuel Hopkins
Uriah Hartley
Philip Hight
Samuel L. Hills
Benjamin F. Hill
Zenas Johnston
Thornton Johnston
Stephen R. Kinnan
John Kenner
John Keener
Stephen R. Kenner
Henry Lambert
Clymer Lindsey
Ira Morris
Joseph Minor
Joseph Morrison
John McKee
George N. Nicely
Joseph Orndoff
Solomon Phillips
Joshua Piles
Thomas B. Roberts
Singleton Roberts
William Ruse
Andrew Rush
Solomon Rose
David Rice

John I. Rinehart
Lewis Russell
Joshua Piles
George W. Reager
John Ruse
Scott L. Rich
Joseph Ridge
Jacob Staley
Jacob Sine
John Sharpnich
Samuel Staley
Israel Shriver
Cavalier Smith
John Sharp
Eli Stickles
Samuel Smith
Edward Smith
William Thompson
John H. Thompson
Benjamin Wilkinson
John D. West
Morgan Wade
James Watson
Henry White
Aaron Walters
Michael Wright
Baldwin Weaver

APPENDIX F: "Teachers' Institute"

The Civil War affected education in Greene County just as it did many other aspects of the county residents' lives. Waynesburg College had been founded by the Cumberland Presbyterian Church in 1849 and chartered by the Commonwealth of Pennsylvania in 1850. The first college building, now referred to as "Hanna Hall," was constructed in 1850-1851. The building cost $5000, and the first classes were held there in November 1851. By 1861, Waynesburg College was beginning to prosper under the leadership of Reverend A. B. Miller, who had graduated from the institution, taught mathematics there, and was appointed president by the board of trustees in 1859. The war, of course, had a major impact on enrollment. Each call for troops issued by the national government drew young men from the advanced classes, resulting in smaller class sizes and fewer graduates. According to Dr. William H. Dusenberry, a small number of Waynesburg College students served in Southern units. As A. B. Miller explained at one time, "Most of our boys fought somewhere during the war, some in the blue, others in the gray."[24] The smallest graduating class was when one student, Rhoda Yeagley, graduated in the commencement exercises for the Class of 1862. Miss Yeagley later married a young man named Edmund Dunn who had been in her class but who had left for the army before the commencement. Dunn eventually became a captain in the Union cavalry. In 1923, the college belatedly conferred a degree on Dunn as of the Class of 1862.[25]

Public education in Greene County was still quite young when the Civil War erupted. Other than informal schools conducted in log cabins, the first formal schools in the county for elementary education were subscription schools, where parents joined together to build or rent a building and pay a teacher. Waynesburg had a subscription school as early as

[24] William H. Dusenberry, *The Waynesburg College Story 1849-1974* (Kent State University Press, 1975), p. 91.
[25] *Ibid.*

1811. Under Pennsylvania's Free School Act of 1834, every township and borough were established as school districts, required to elect a school board, and provide free public education. By 1837, there were free public schools in Cumberland, Franklin, Jefferson, Marion, Morgan, Morris, Monongahela, and Richhill Townships. In 1854, Pennsylvania created the office of State Superintendant of Common Schools as well as the office of county superintendant of schools. Charles A. Black, Democrat from Greene County, served as the first state superintendant by virtue of his position as Secretary of the Commonwealth that year. The first Greene County Superintendant of Schools was John A. Gordon, who served from 1854 until he marched off to war as captain of the Pursley Guards in the fall of 1861. At that time, A. B. Miller served as county superintendant until replaced by T. J. Teal in 1863.[26]

Both Miller and Teal reported the sad effect the war had on the county's already strained support for public education. In the 1862-1863 school year, Miller noted the "vulgar and unreasonable practice" of "barring-out the teacher" was common in several districts. Such actions were condemned as "the occasion of quarrels, loss of time, destruction of school property, and disgraceful conduct." He added, however, that the common school system was gaining favor in the county, although "ignorance and prejudice wear away slowly."[27] Both Miller and Teal commented that irregular attendance was a problem in many county schools. Part of this was due to the presence of serious disease like diphtheria, but other problems included parents keeping children home for "light and trivial causes" and a lack of skill in some teachers causing a lack of interest in school.[28] Both men noted, however, the beneficial influence brought to Greene County education by the presence of Waynesburg College. In addition, Miller referred to Greene Academy in Carmichaels as a "light shining in a dark place." The Academy had done a yeoman's service in providing education for students beyond the eight grades of public

[26] Smith, pp. 21-22.
[27] *Report of the Superintendant of Common Schools of Pennsylvania for the Year ending June 4, 1863* (Harrisburg: Singerly & Myers, state printers, 1864), p. 93.
[28] *State Superintendant's Report for the Year Ending June 4, 1864*, p. 134.

education. Having served out its usefulness during the Civil War years, in March 1865, in accordance with state law, the trustees deeded the property to Carmichaels Borough School District. The building was used as a public school until 1893.[29]

At least part of the problem with teachers' skills in the Greene County schools was attributable to the war. Military service took away many of the best teachers. In addition, some districts, no doubt because of rising expenses and to meet soldier bounty obligations, were forced to lower teaching wages. There was a resulting scarcity of teachers in some areas that compelled school directors to employ persons with inferior qualifications. As Superintendant Teal noted in his report to the state for the year ending June 1, 1864:

> The great conflict, which has been raging for the last three years, has had a deleterious effect upon the cause of education. Many of the ablest and most successful teachers have been called from their peaceful professions to fields of carnage and strife. Some fill soldiers' graves, on distant fields; others are still in the ranks of war.[30]

One method of trying to improve the teaching qualifications of those teachers who remained in the county was the "Teachers' Institute." In January 1862, County School Superintendant A. B. Miller announced that the teachers of Greene County were requested to meet in Waynesburg on January 30th at seven o'clock P.M. for the organization of a permanent county institute. As Miller explained:

> The object is to organize, for your good, an association which will be under your own control. I will make all necessary arrangements for the first meeting and will do all in my power to render it interesting and profitable. The exercises will consist of class drills, essays, discussions, etc.[31]

---

[29] *State Superintendant's Report for the Year Ending June 4, 1863*, p. 93; Smith, p. 23.

[30] *State Superintendant's report for the Year Ending June 4, 1864*, p. 135

[31] *Waynesburg Messenger*, 22 January 1862, p. 3.

Some topics suggested for this organizational meeting included discussions regarding exercises for close of a school term, banishment of the rod from the classroom, the age when pupils should begin reading, and whether students should study silently or "in a whisper." The institute was scheduled to last from Tuesday evening until Saturday afternoon, and it was reported that some township school directors were willing to pay teachers for their time if they attended.[32]

Several townships also had district teachers' institutes. In 1862, Miller reported that only one district held a successful institute, but the next year all the districts except two made efforts at holding institutes. Although not as successful as he had hoped, Miller was certain a beginning had been made that would insure success by the next term.[33] Miller proved correct and Teal reported that in 1863-1864, district teachers' institutes were generally organized throughout the county. The teachers were for the most part favorable to the organizations, although directors in some districts lacked much enthusiasm for the project.[34] Still, teachers' institutes became a fixture in Greene County education over the next century.

An excellent example of a district institute was the Richhill Teachers' Institute held February 28, 1863. The teachers met at the school house in Jacksonville (Wind Ridge). Newton Braddock served as President, Miss M. E. Boyd as Vice President, and C. Carson Chambers as Secretary. The meeting discussed three subjects. C. Carson Chambers gave a presentation on the use of the rod in school. Chambers talked about both the use and abuse of the rod, concluding that the least amount of discipline needed to maintain order in the classroom was the best. School government was discussed by Thomas J. McCleary. He noted that the only purpose of school government is to maintain order and that "no rule of action can be laid down to suit every emergency" and "that circumstances must determine or at least modify every action in school government." McCleary explained to his audience that

---

[32] *Ibid.*

[33] *Report of State Superintendant for Year Ending June 4, 1862,* p. 94; *State Report for Year Ending June 4, 1863,* p. 92.

[34] *Report of State Superintendant for Year Ending June 4, 1864,* p. 134.

"education is a drawing out, a leading process, and consequently that we cannot drive learning into the mind." The final speaker, William B. Teagarden, a thirty-year veteran teacher, concluded the program by giving a defense of the use of the rod and then discussing the rise and progress of common schools. Teagarden was apparently a gifted speaker and had much to say on his subject from his own experience. This was the fourth meeting of the Richhill Township Teachers' Institute, and it was noted in the published minutes that the institute planned to meet once per month after the closing of school throughout the spring and summer months.[35]

---

[35] *Waynesburg Messenger,* 25 March 1863, p. 1.

APPENDIX G: Greene County Medal of Honor Recipients

At least six men from Greene County who served in the Union army were awarded Congressional Medals of Honor. Created by a Congressional resolution on July 12, 1862, the Medal of Honor was awarded during the Civil War to a soldier who distinguished himself by conspicuous gallantry and intrepidity at the risk of his life above and beyond the call of duty. Greene County men receiving the medal for service in the Civil War included the following:

James Pipes, Company A, 140th Pennsylvania Infantry, was awarded the medal for actions taken at Gettysburg on July 2, 1863, and at Reams Station, Virginia, on August 25, 1864. At Gettysburg, Pipes, then a sergeant, while withdrawing in the face of a rapid advance of the Confederates in the Wheatfield, assisted First Lieutenant James J. Purman in moving a wounded and helpless comrade to safety. At Reams Station, while commanding a skirmish line, Pipes voluntarily assisted in stopping a flank movement by the enemy. In both actions, Pipes was severely wounded. His wound at Reams Station caused him to lose an arm.

James J. Purman, Company A, 140th Pennsylvania Infantry, received the medal for his action at Gettysburg in the Wheatfield on July 2, 1863, in removing a wounded man to safety, with the assistance of Sergeant James Pipes, during a withdrawal and while under heavy fire from the enemy. Lieutenant Purman was also severely wounded and lost his left leg.

William E. Leonard, Company F, 85th Pennsylvania Infantry, from Jacksonville, Greene County (Wind Ridge), received the medal for his action in capturing a Confederate battle flag at Deep Bottom, Virginia, on

April 16, 1864.

John Shanes, Company K, 14th (West) Virginia Volunteer Infantry, from Brave, was awarded the medal for his actions during a skirmish at Carter's Farm, Virginia, where his regiment suffered twenty men killed and fifty-two wounded.

Charles A. Swan, while serving in Company K, 4th Iowa Cavalry, received the medal for his action at Selma, Alabama, on April 2, 1865, in capturing the flag bearer and the colors of the 11th Mississippi, C. S. A.

Andrew J. Young, Company F, 1st Pennsylvania Cavalry, from Carmichaels, was awarded the medal for his action in capturing a Confederate battle flag at Paines Crossroads, Virginia, on April 5, 1865.

BIBLIOGRAPHY

Newspapers:
Beaver Radical
Columbia Spy (Columbia, PA)
Daily Evening Bulletin (Philadelphia, PA)
Daily Intelligencer (Wheeling, WV)
Daily Morning Post (Pittsburgh, PA)
Daily Patriot and Union (Harrisburg, PA)
Franklin Repository (Chambersburg, PA)
Genius of Liberty (Uniontown, PA)
Greene County Republican
Huntingdon Globe
Journal of the Telegraph (Western Union Telegraph Company)
Lancaster Intelligencer
Lehigh Register
Pennsylvania Daily Telegraph (Harrisburg, PA)
Pittsburgh Daily Gazette and Advertiser
The Pittsburgh Post
The Press (Philadelphia, PA)
The Reporter and Tribune (Washington, PA)
Republican Compiler (Gettysburg, PA)
The Waynesburg Independent
Waynesburg Messenger
Weekly Mariettian (Marietta, PA)
Woman's Centennial Paper (Waynesburg, PA)

Manuscripts and Archives:

Clerk of Court's Office, Greene County Courthouse, Waynesburg, PA, records of *Commonwealth v. Thomas Phillips,* #7 December Sessions 1864.

Hopkins, D. S. "Reminiscence of My Service in the U. S. Army from 26th Day of February 1864 to 11th Day of July 1865," PA Historical & Museum Commission, Division of Archives and Manuscripts, MG-6-Diaries and Journals-Box #1.

J. F. McCullough Post 367 of the G. A. R., "Memorial Day 1908 Waynesburg, PA, Souvenir Program."

Abraham Lincoln Papers at the Library of Congress, Series I, General Correspondence, 1833-1916.

Lincoln, Abraham. *Collected Works*, Vol. 3. Rutgers University Press, 1953.

Lindsey Family Letters, Archives of Greene County Historical Society, Waynesburg, PA.

Lindsey, Honorable James. "Diary," Cornerstone Genealogical Society, Waynesburg, PA.

Mildred Family Letters, private collection of D. Kent Fonner, Beach Lake, PA.

MLR to Cousin Neddy, letter dated 20 November 1864 in private collection of Dr. Thomas Pavick, Waynesburg University, Waynesburg, PA.

Scherich, Isaac. "The 18th Pennsylvania Rides Again!!," transcription of the journal of Private Isaac Scherich, Company A, 18th Pennsylvania Cavalry, Cornerstone Genealogical Society: Waynesburg, PA (original in Trans-Appalachian Room, Waynesburg University Library, Waynesburg, PA).

Silveus Family Letters, private collection of D. Kent Fonner, Beach Lake, PA.

White, Henry Solomon. "Abstract of Diary Kept by Henry Solomon White in the Period Between September 1861 and June 1865," Cornerstone Genealogical Society, Waynesburg, PA.

Government Publications:

The Congressional Globe, 37th Congress-38th Congress.

Washington, D.C.: Government Printing Office, 1863-1864.

Journal of the House of Representatives of the Commonwealth of Pennsylvania, of the Session Begun at Harrisburg, on the Sixth Day of January, 1863. Harrisburg: Singerly & Myers, State Printers, 1863.

Kennedy, Joseph C. G., Superintendent of Census. *Agriculture of the United States in 1860; Compiled from the Original Returns of the 8th Census under the Direction of the Secretary of the Interior.* Washington, D. C.: Government Printing Office, 1864.

Kennedy, Joseph C. G., Superintendent of Census. *Population of the United States in 1860; Compiled from the Original Returns of the 8th Census under Direction of the Secretary of the Interior.* Washington, D.C.: Government Printing Office, 1864.

Kneedler v. Lane, 45 PA Reports 238 (PA Supreme Court 1863).

Official Records of the War of the Rebellion, Series I-III. Washington, D.C.: Government Printing Office, 1889.

Pennsylvania Historical Records Survey Division of Professional and Service Projects, Works Projects Administration. *Inventory of the County Archives of Pennsylvania: Greene County,* #30. Waynesburg, PA: Board of County Commissioners, 1940.

Report of the Superintendent of Common Schools of Pennsylvania for the Year Ending June 1, 1864. Harrisburg: Singerly & Myers, State Printers, 1865.

Report of the Transactions of the Pennsylvania State Agricultural Society for the Years 1861-'62-'63, Vol. VI. Harrisburg: Singerly & Myers, State Printers, 1863.

Stone, Ralph W. and Frederick G. Clapp, *Oil and Gas Fields of*

Greene County, PA. Washington, D.C.: Government Printing Office, 1907.

United States. *Manufactures of the United States in 1860; Compiled from the Original Returns of the 8th Census under the Direction of the Secretary of the Interior.* Washington, D. C.: Government Printing Office, 1865.

_____. *Register of Officers and Agents, Civil, Military, and Naval, in the Service of the United States, on the Thirtieth September, 1861.* Washington, D. C.: Government Printing Office, 1862.

Regimental Histories:

Bates, Samuel P. *History of Pennsylvania Volunteers,* 5 Vols. Harrisburg: B. Singerly, State Printer, 1869.

Dickey, Luther S. *History of the Eighty-fifth Regiment Pennsylvania Volunteer Infantry, 1861-1865.* New York, 1915.

Eberly, Robert E. *Bouquets from the Cannon's Mouth: Soldiering with the 8th Regiment of the Pennsylvania Reserves.* Shippensburg, PA: White Mane Books, 2004.

Farrar, Samuel Clarke. *The Twenty-Second Pennsylvania Cavalry and the Ringgold Battalion, 1861-1865.* Pittsburgh: The New Werner Company, 1911.

Kirk, Charles H. *History of the Fifteenth Pennsylvania Volunteer Cavalry: Which was Recruited and Known as the Anderson Cavalry in the Rebellion of 1861-1865.* Philadelphia, 1906.

Lloyd, William P. *History of the First Regiment Pennsylvania Reserve Cavalry.* Philadelphia, 1864.

O'Brien, Katherine. *The Seventh West Virginia Volunteer Infantry,* Thesis Submitted for M. A. in the Faculty of the Graduate School of West Virginia University, Morgantown,

WV, 1965.

Publication Committee of the Regimental Association, ed. *History of the Eighteenth Regiment of Cavalry Pennsylvania Volunteers, (163d Regiment of the Line) 1862-1865.* New York: Wynkoop Hallendbeck Crawford Co., 1909.

Stewart, D. D., Professor Robert Laird. *History of the One Hundred and Fortieth Regiment Pennsylvania Volunteers.* 140th Pennsylvania Regimental Association, 1912.

Secondary Works and Articles:

Albright, Rebecca Gifford. "The Civil War Career of Andrew Gregg Curtin, Governor of Pennsylvania," *Western Pennsylvania Historical Society Magazine,* Vol. 47, No. 4 (October 1964).

Antill, Nancy Simms. "A Bibliography of Greene County, Pennsylvania," Greene County Historical Society Library. Unpublished paper for West Virginia University Library Science 410, 1978-1979.

Bates, Samuel P. *History of Greene County, Pennsylvania.* Chicago: Nelson, Rishforth, and Co., 1888.

Bausman, Joseph Henderson and John Samuel Duss. *History of Beaver County, Pennsylvania, and its centennial celebration.* New York: Knickerbocker Press, 1904.

Boehm, Robert B. "The Jones-Imboden Raid through West Virginia," *Civil War Times Illustrated,* Vol. 3, No. 2 (May 1964).

Bradley, Erwin S. *Triumph of Militant Republicanism: A Study of Pennsylvania and Presidential Politics, 1860-1872.* Philadelphia: University of Pennsylvania Press, 1964.

Crumrine, Boyd. *The Courts of Justice, Bench and Bar of*

Washington County, Pennsylvania. Chicago: R. R. Donelley and Sons, 1902.

Davis, Stanton L. *Pennsylvania Politics, 1860-1863.* Cleveland, Ohio: Western Reserve University, 1935.

Dusenberry, William H. *The Waynesburg College Story 1849-1974.* Kent, Ohio: The Kent State University Press, 1975.

_____. "Nineteenth Century Transportation in Greene County," *Greene Hills Echo* (Greene County Historical Society, Waynesburg, PA), Vol. VI, No. 4 (December 1976).

Evans, Lewis K. *Pioneer History of Greene County.* Waynesburg: Waynesburg Republican, 1941.

Fonner, D. Kent. "A Brief History of Oil and Gas Development in Greene County, Pennsylvania (1861-1930)," Cornerstone Genealogical Society Library, Waynesburg, PA. Unpublished manuscript, 2000.

_____. "'Dear Mary:' The Civil War Letters of William Silveus," *Cornerstone Clues: Quarterly Journal of the Cornerstone Genealogical Society,* Vol. XX, No. 1 (February 1995).

_____. "An Investigation into Antiwar Sentiment in Greene County, Pennsylvania (1861-1865)," *Cornerstone Clues,* 5 parts, Vol. XXVII, No. 1-Vol. XXVIII, No. 1 (February 2002-February 2003).

_____. "'We Had Quite an Exciting Time . . . :' James Lindsey at the 1857 State Democratic Convention," *Cornerstone Clues,* Vol. XXIV, No. 3 (August 1999).

Hanna, Rev. William. *History of Greene County, Pa.* 1882.

Hyman, Harold M. *A More Perfect Union: The Impact of the Civil War and Reconstruction on the Constitution.* Boston: Houghton Mifflin Company, 1975.

187

James, Alfred P. "The Significance of Western Pennsylvania in American History," *Western Pennsylvania Historical Magazine,* Vol. 16, No. 4 (November 1933).

Jepsen, Thomas C. *My Sisters Telegraphic: Women in the Telegraph Office, 1846-1950.* Athens, Ohio: Ohio University Press, 2000.

Jordon, John W. and James Hadden, ed. *Genealogical and Personal History of Fayette and Greene Counties Pennsylvania,* 3 vols. New York: Lewis Historical Publishing Company, 1912.

Lang, Theodore F. *Loyal West Virginia from 1861 to 1865.* Baltimore, MD: The Deutsch Publishing Co., 1895.

"Letters from a Civil War Soldier" (G. Wm. Pratt), *Cornerstone Clues,* Vol. XXIV, No. 1 (February 1999).

Longacre, Edward G. *Mounted Raids of the Civil War.* New York: A.S. Barnes and Company, 1975.

McClure, Alexander Kelly. *Old Time Notes of Pennsylvania,* 2 Vols. Philadelphia: The John C. Winston Company, 1905.

McConnell, J. L. *McConnell's Map of Greene County Pennsylvania.* Philadelphia: Tuttle & Co., 1865 (reprint and compilation by Cornerstone Genealogical Society, Waynesburg, PA, in 1977).

Neely, Jr., Mark E. "The Civil War and the Two Party System," James M. McPherson, ed., *"We Cannot Escape History:" Abraham Lincoln and the Last Best Hope of Earth.* Chicago: University of Illinois Press, 1995.

_____. *The Fate of Liberty: Abraham Lincoln and Civil Liberties.* New York: Oxford University Press, 1991.

_____. *The Union Divided: Party Conflict in the Civil*

War North. Cambridge, MA: Harvard University Press, 2002.

Palladino, Grace. *Another Civil War: Labor, Capital, and the State in the Anthracite Regions of Pennsylvania, 1840-1868.* New York: Fordham University Press, 2006.

Powell, Marie Elaine, "All These Munificent Gifts . . . the Social and Economic development of Greene County, Pennsylvania 1760-1976," Greene County Historical Society Library. Unpublished manuscript of Honors Project submitted to Denison University, 5 May 1976.

Randall, J. G. *Constitutional Problems under Lincoln.* New York: D. Appleton & Company, 1926.

Rodearmel, William. *Portraits of the Heads of State and Sketches of Members of the Legislature of Pennsylvania 1893-1894.* Harrisburg: E. K. Myers Printing Houses, 1893.

Sandow, Robert M. *Deserter Country: Civil War Opposition in the Pennsylvania Appalachians.* New York: Fordham University Press, 2009.

Sauers, Dr. Richard, ed. *The Bloody 85th: The Letters of Milton McJunkin, a Western Pennsylvania Soldier in the Civil War.* Lynchburg, VA: Schroeder Publications, 2002.

Shankman, Arnold. "Draft Resistance in Civil War Pennsylvania," *Pennsylvania Magazine of History and Biography,* Vol. 101, No. 2 (April 1977).

_____. *The Pennsylvania Antiwar Movement, 1861-1865.* Rutherford, N. J.: Fairleigh Dickinson University Press, 1980.

Smith, Dr. G. Wayne. *History of Greene County, Pennsylvania,* 2 Vols. Morgantown, WV: Cornerstone Genealogical Society of Waynesburg, PA, 1996.

Sypher, J. R. *History of the Pennsylvania Reserve Corps.*

Lancaster, PA: Elias Barr & Co., 1865.

Turner, George A. *Civil War Letters from Soldiers and Citizens of Columbia County, Pennsylvania.* New York: American Heritage Custom Publishing, 1996.

Waychoff, Andrew J. *Local History of Greene County and Southwestern Pennsylvania.* Waynesburg, 1975.

Weber, Jennifer L. *Copperheads: The Rise and Fall of Lincoln's Opponents in the North.* New York: Oxford University Press, 2006.

White, Jonathan W. "A Pennsylvania Judge Views the Rebellion: the Civil War Letters of George Washington Woodward," *Pennsylvania Magazine of History and Biography,* Vol. 129, No. 2 (April 2005).

Internet Resources:

Biographical Directory of the United States Congress, 1774-Present, http://bioguide.congress.gov/biosearch/biosearch.asp, retrieved 10 July 2011.

Davison, Bill A., transcriber. "Trial of the Negroes" from *Waynesburg Messenger* dated 29 December 1859, *A History of Slavery and People of Color in Greene County and Southwest Pennsylvania,* http://home.comcast.net/~janslater/Waynesburg_Messenger_Trial_Coverage.htm, retrieved 21 August 2011.

"Pennsylvania Volunteers of the Civil War – Greene County Medal of Honor Recipients," http://www.pacivilwar.com/medalofhonor/greene.html, retrieved 9 March 2012.

INDEX

ABOUT THE AUTHOR

D. Kent Fonner was born in Greene County, Pennsylvania, the son of Henry B. Fonner and Helen (Jacobs) Fonner. He is a graduate of Waynesburg College and has a Master of Arts degree in history from Duquesne University in Pittsburgh. In addition, Mr. Fonner also has a Juris Doctor degree from the University of Pittsburgh School of Law. He has previously published historical articles in *The Pennsylvania Magazine of History and Biography, America's Civil War, Military History,* and the Cornerstone Genealogical Society's *Cornerstone Clues.* Articles written by Mr. Fonner about his grandfather, Waynesburg ornithologist and oologist J. Warren Jacobs, were published in the Purple Martin Conservation Association's journal, *The Purple Martin Update,* and *Florida Wildlife.* Mr. Fonner's research on the collapse of the Farmers and Drovers National Bank of Waynesburg, Pennsylvania, appears in Volume I of Eric Monkkonen's *Crime and Justice in American History.* He has taught college courses in history and criminal justice at Waynesburg College, Mount Aloysius College in Cresson, Pennsylvania, and Northampton Community College at the Monroe County campus in Tannersville, Pennsylvania. Mr. Fonner currently lives in northeastern Pennsylvania with his wife, Diane.

14742602R00111

Made in the USA
Charleston, SC
28 September 2012